Teaching Life Skills in the School Library

Teaching Life Skills in the School Library

Career, Finance, and Civic Engagement in a Changing World

Blanche Woolls and
Connie Hamner Williams

LIBRARIES
UNLIMITED™
An Imprint of ABC-CLIO, LLC
Santa Barbara, California • Denver, Colorado

Library of Congress Cataloging-in-Publication Data

Names: Woolls, Blanche, author. | Hamner Williams, Connie, author.
Title: Teaching life skills in the school library : career, finance, and
  civic engagement in a changing world / Blanche Woolls and Connie Hamner
  Williams.
Description: Santa Barbara, California : Libraries Unlimited, [2019] |
  Includes bibliographical references and index.
Identifiers: LCCN 2018043994 (print) | LCCN 2018053086 (ebook) | ISBN
  9781440868900 (ebook) | ISBN 9781440868894 (paperback : acid-free paper)
Subjects: LCSH: School libraries—Activity programs—United States. | School
  librarian participation in curriculum planning—United States. | Life
  skills—Study and teaching—Activity programs. | Libraries and education.
Classification: LCC Z675.S3 (ebook) | LCC Z675.S3 W875 2019 (print) | DDC
  027.8—dc23
LC record available at https://lccn.loc.gov/2018043994

ISBN: 978–1–4408–6889–4 (paperback)
      978–1–4408–6890–0 (ebook)

23 22 21 20 19   1 2 3 4 5

This book is also available as an eBook.

Libraries Unlimited
An Imprint of ABC-CLIO, LLC

ABC-CLIO, LLC
147 Castilian Drive
Santa Barbara, California 93117
www.abc-clio.com

This book is printed on acid-free paper ∞

Manufactured in the United States of America

This book is dedicated to Miriam Lykke, an ESL teacher for many years at Senn High School in Chicago whose mantra was "Never borrow money to pay for education. Instead research ways to get scholarships, go to a college you can afford to attend, work to earn the tuition before you enroll, or work while you go to class," and to my granddaughter, Laura Woolls, and her three Georgetown roommates, Deserea Brio, Frankie Rubio, and Julie Zovak, who continue to share family and friends after they have finished that step in their lives. They are examples of how to follow Miriam's edict.

—Blanche

Dedicated to all the librarians who step out of their comfort zone to try new things, who share their wisdom widely, and who support others as we all take those courageous steps to bring information, imagination, and serendipity to each and every student we encounter. Thank you, each and every one of you.

—Connie

Contents

Preface

This book encourages school librarians to think about the many ways that they can help students successfully clear the many hurdles they encounter through their years in K–12 education along the way toward that diploma. This kind of student support goes beyond the role of managing the room in the school called many different names, from "library" through "media center" and "learning commons." It goes beyond helping students learn to read and enjoy reading and goes well beyond teaching them how to become information literate. It goes beyond those lessons librarians teach, as a part of a directed unit of instruction, when classes come to the library with their teachers. It moves into very different ways to use your library to help students grow.

In asking you to consider taking on these new assignments that might not fit easily into your already busy day, you will find an icon that indicates an activity to help you implement the text. These activities are found at the end of each chapter. Many of them can be done almost as an aside to your other plans with students. Others will require working with another teacher or the guidance counselor, and yet others will require administrative support. What is most important is that students learn from their earliest time in school how to be prepared for life after graduation.

By providing additional programming opportunities, those activities given during student "off" time from recess in elementary to study hall in the upper grades, lunch hour, and before and after school, you are introducing students to the many "real-life" issues they face as they move through the grades toward graduation and when they step into that real world.

This book shares activities from school library colleagues, from government and educational sources, from observations and programming at conference, as well as from personal experiences. The bibliography at the end of the book includes the resources mentioned in the book and other information that will be helpful to you as you continue your efforts to collaborate with your teachers, your administration, and your community to help your students prepare for the challenge of being an adult. The activities and the bibliography are designed to encourage you to think about the proposed ideas, try them out as they are, or modify them before you begin. You are invited to contact your authors with any questions you may have about your plans and to share your successes so we can help you share them widely: Blanche Woolls (blanche.woolls@sjsu.edu) and Connie Williams (chwms@mac.com).

You may have your own ideas for helping your students find ways around obstacles in their path with a different kind of instruction. You need to share those successes with your colleagues both locally and nationally. Prepare a presentation for your school district librarians and teachers or your state library conference. This book encourages school librarians to do all that they can to prepare every student to make it to graduation well prepared for the wide world that awaits him or her. It means taking that leadership role in the school to show the importance of reaching all children with the message that they can succeed and you are there to help them.

Chapter 1

Leading Students into Their Future after High School

Children starting school today are entering a world that is in constant flux. Politics, the environment, immigration, and other important issues are topics that confront them from many vantage points. Many students are deeply involved in these issues themselves, while others hear and see the conversations going on through television or social media. Television can offer varying perspectives, and if parents watch the news on different channels, children may see many versions of events. In a perfect world, parents and children would be discussing these events after listening, viewing, and reading about them in a variety of media. However, fewer children watch their parents reading the printed newspaper, because fewer adults read the newspaper today. "As of early 2016, just two-in-ten U.S. adults often get news from print newspapers. This has fallen from 27% in 2013."[1] Many television channels and other media, including social media, easily offer a "filter bubble" that gives one perspective, making it incumbent upon viewers today to know and understand the mission and goals for those television news and other programming channels. Looking for those programs and newspapers, either online or in print, offering an editorial process that includes editing and content checking, viewers can begin to weigh in on the facts that are reported and make personal decisions on where and how they might want to act upon that news.

Social media is ever present and available to almost every man, woman, and child, across the income and education spectrum.[2] While the platforms vary by age, teens like different apps than what their parents like, and the information from these sources is seldom vetted by an authority and most often reflects only the perceptions of the person keying in the text. It makes it difficult for anyone to separate fact from fiction, true from false, or the lie in any post.

Helping students learn to question what they hear and read has become the responsibility of every teacher. This is a difficult addition to an already cramped curriculum teachers must teach as mandated and defined by their school, district, state, and in some instances national educational leadership. They have little time to do more than complete the assigned textbook and worry about results of the required tests, which may, in those districts where pay is aligned to test results, ultimately affect their salaries. Because many students never take courses where topics such as financial planning, interpersonal relations, or community engagement are offered, this places a large gap in the lives of students who need to be prepared for life after they leave high school. It also provides a great opportunity for the school librarian.

The challenges facing students today are quite different from those facing previous generations. Manufacturing jobs have disappeared with the advent of robots or other industrial technologies that replace human labor, and many more have disappeared with the relocation of factories out of state or out of the country. They have felt their grandparents' and parents' concerns about their salaries, job duties, or even the certainty that their jobs will continue to exist. Knowing that they will need a good job, students still need to define what "good" means in today's ever-changing world. These students need a realistic picture of their opportunities, especially if they are disinterested in school and do not seem to find a compelling reason to stay. Should their absenteeism increase because of disenfranchisement with the system, they move further and further backward from obtaining that "good" job. Remaining in school means understanding what further education is needed to obtain that first job and how to remain relevant when needed skills for good jobs change.

Along with understanding the requirements for that good job and the cost of living in any environment, financial awareness is critical for students to manage their income and resources after high school. The cost of living in relation to that income requires careful planning to maintain adequate housing and food while allowing something additional for clothing, transportation, and recreation.

In addition to career planning for that good job and laying the groundwork for strong financial awareness, students need to be actively involved in learning about the importance of choosing those who will be establishing and enforcing the laws that govern them at all levels. The first steps include becoming aware of their responsibility to become informed citizens in our democracy and then understanding their role in the election process by selecting the best possible candidates. They must become confident and engaged citizens within their community, helping to build and maintain the infrastructure that supports the common good. Democracy can be fragile, and as such, it is not acceptable for citizens to be passive receptors of information. Today's communication glut brings so much information to organize and research for understanding that students and adults must actively pay attention to the sources and the varying perspectives before participating in community action or acting upon them by voting. This kind of active research is accomplished by delving deeper than what students can often find at home or through their social media choices. Creating the future citizen who is willing and eager to solve problems through active participation is a primary focus for today's education.

Responsibilities for the School Librarian

School librarians are well placed to create, as their primary goal, the instruction and support of student engagement in their democracy by understanding their role in protecting it at all costs. Librarians have always been at the forefront in the fight for freedom of information. They protect and continue to disseminate information for all, as shown through the Library Bill of Rights,[3] and they demonstrate this continually through library organization, collection development, and within the topics of instruction they teach, including information literacy, good digital citizenship, and equal access of all resources. They also reinforce any lessons learned in the classrooms that move students into adulthood, understanding and accepting their roles in this society by coteaching, collaborating, and targeted activities to support that classroom learning.

Because you and your library are at the center of learning, you have many opportunities to work with all the teachers and students in your building. You support your classroom colleagues in their efforts to complete their curriculum units by providing the scaffolding for students to learn the skills that accompany that content knowledge. When the library serves students beyond class periods and also during lunch breaks, tutorials, and before and after school, you have opportunities to develop activities that can bring interesting people and activities into the library: speakers from the community, author visits, and maker activities, among others, all engaging activities that help to open doors for students. Encouraging students to read both for their own enjoyment and for finding information is, of course, another wonderful way you help bring ideas and open doors for your students. Creating lifelong readers supports the engagement and confidence to become lifelong participants in democracy. Every school librarian is uniquely positioned to help students prepare for their adult lives after they have completed high school.

While the ideas of career planning, community engagement, voting, citizenship, and financial well-being seem easily aligned to a high school curriculum, these topics really need to begin in the elementary school and continue steadily through middle, junior high, and high school. Being able to graduate students who are ready to move into the next stage of their journey to adulthood begins with that first day of school as a preschool or kindergarten student and continues each day of each year until they graduate.

To help with this, chapters begin with the responsibility of the librarian in four areas. These areas include the education environment, career information, economic awareness, and civic responsibility, and they are expanded later in the chapter.

Education Environment describes how students live within the structure of their school. Elementary is typically a single teacher, while secondary changes to multiple classes with single subjects and many teachers. Students are prepared within each school year for each next step in the continuum and what the expectations will be at that level. This book discusses what happens when they move out of the "safety" of the single classroom environment to take the responsibility for moving from one class to the next and when it becomes your task as well as that of the classroom teacher to help students consider questions about their lives such as "What is my goal: Do I choose higher education, or will I attend some technical training, or will I make sure that the courses I take in high school prepare me for a career immediately after I graduate? Will an internship help me identify my goals and help me network within a chosen field?" Helping students develop their plans is a first step in this continuum.

Plans are useful to help lay a foundation, create a focus, and give personal guidelines to follow. As students go through their K–12 years, they will have many plans. In the early grades, they may say they want to be an actor, a pilot, or a firefighter. Those plans may change as they go through the grades and discover new skills, interests, and talents. The Plan A of the later high school years includes those decisions they are making about higher education, apprenticeships, work, or travel. Having a plan is really not much more than creating a path to follow or a goal to work toward, which includes creating the environment to reach those goals and walk those paths. After high school, most will change those plans many times, creating then Plans

Plan A

One family told their children in high school, "You have to have a plan. It doesn't have to be a great plan, and you may change it—but you have to have one while you are in school." They called it Plan A. As their children went through school, they participated in activities, interests, and goals that interested them. Then, they were to follow through by choosing classes and attending the sports or other activity they had chosen. It turned out that none of the children had a career in mind, and so they did not have career paths that they particularly wanted to follow; they just knew that college was next as their parents strongly encouraged them to assume that as a next step. They worked hard, experimented with courses, and involved themselves in extracurricular activities. In college, through the years, these young adults changed their "plans," one starting out as a history major that turned into anthropology and that then turned into law. Their friends' lives took different paths as they too went through life. Many changed careers after several years in their first Plan A. Only one person is remembered who, 45 years after graduation from high school, is still working with Plan A and who still loves his job as much as he did in the beginning.

B, C, D, or more. While it is useful to have a plan, a goal, it is changeable when circumstances warrant and, as one builds skills, allows the creation of new opportunities to follow. As different doors open, decisions to walk on through can open up whole new opportunities.

Working with the guidance counselor, you and the information students find in the library will be central to their development of plans. Resources in the library offer students the facts and figures they need to make decisions about their plans, the training they will need and the best place to go to get that education, the requirements for enrolling, the length of time for the courses, and the costs.

Career Information provides students with choices of what they might like to be doing as an adult and then discover what they must learn in order to do that kind of work. This type of information includes career discovery as well as self-interest exploration. In their early years, students observe that there are many kinds of jobs available to them. They are given time to explore those jobs and what it takes to get to them: schooling, interviewing, interning, and networking. As students go through school, they need to gain the skills that help them identify job possibilities, seek strategies for fulfilling requirements, and follow through to a positive outcome.

Economic Awareness provides students with instruction in financial literacy. As all students progress through the grades, they need to learn about the challenges of finances involved in being an adult such as opening a checking account and the cost when one does not maintain an adequate balance, budgeting for necessities such as groceries and rent, the percentage assessed for credit card debt, and even the arithmetic of purchasing a home.

This introduction to the world of economics and finances is very important in this complicated, information-rich world. Starting in elementary school, students need to gain and practice math skills that give them a firm foundation for making the financial decisions that will impact their lives. As they move through the grades, math-skill knowledge opens the door to economic understanding, including how what happens in the world impacts personal decisions. Learning how their adult lives will need adequate financial compensation for work they accomplish so that they can purchase the things they want and not just the things they need is of great importance for everyone.

Civic Responsibility involves giving students a sense of their responsibilities as citizens and what will be required of them. Many agree that schools no longer teach "civics" and students are not well prepared to understand governance. The Brown Center on Education Policy at Brookings seems to agree:

> A growing sentiment holds that many of the country's greatest challenges today relate to the state of its politics, with implications for the cohesion of American society and functioning of its democracy. However, even as politics increasingly penetrate American classrooms, U.S. education policy—as implemented in state accountability systems, for

example—continues to emphasize students' performance in mathematics and reading as the dominant focus of K-12 schooling. To the extent this emphasis has crowded out a focus on students' civic development, we should ask whether today's schools are, in fact, responsive to the needs of our time.[4]

The question about whether schools are responsive to the needs of our time brings up another debate topic: Was civics or social studies a loser when it was not a direct focus of No Child Left Behind? Are schools making up for this? Emily Cardinali suggests some states are beginning to do just that:

> Fake news. Record-low voting turnout. Frequent and false claims from elected officials. Vitriol in many corners of political debate.
>
> These are symptoms we hear of all the time that our democracy is not so healthy.
>
> And those factors might be why many states are turning to the traditional—and obvious—place where people learn how government is supposed to work: schools. More than half of the states in their last legislative sessions—27 to be exact—have considered bills or other proposals to expand the teaching of civics.[5]

If your state is one of the 27, your seniors may be required to take the test given to immigrants who are applying for citizenship. If so, you can collaborate with your civics teachers to help students study for this, and school librarians can also begin some of this preparation in other years so this is not something really unfamiliar. Cardinali shares the findings to help understand where this information is lacking:

> In 2014, just 22 percent of eighth-graders scored "proficient" on the civics part of the National Assessment of Educational Progress (NAEP), commonly called the "Nation's Report Card." The test is graded based on achievement rather than on a pass-fail basis. That same year, 26 percent scored "below basic."
>
> If students are "proficient," they can probably explain the purpose of government, recognize the importance of the rule of law, and understand the separation of power among branches of the government. At the "basic" level, students should be able to identify the fundamental principles of American democracy and the documents that make up that foundation, plus they should understand the different rights and responsibilities U.S. citizens have.[6]

Collaborating with your elementary teachers who cover social studies and history as well as the junior and senior high teachers who have classes in U.S. history and civics, you can begin to encourage information-seeking activities to help with understanding as well as asking students to help create bulletin boards, posters, and other visuals to make fundamental principles and our foundation documents, from the Declaration of Independence and the U.S. Constitution with its Bill of Rights to the latest effort for Congress to repeal a law. For students to understand our governance structure and their civic responsibility is a part of your assignment; you are there to provide them with the information they need if your school is not dedicating time, curriculum, and activities toward that end. It goes beyond just knowing about the governance structure; it is the responsibility of any citizen of the United States to be informed on the issues being discussed with governmental bodies at all levels: city, state, and national. Knowing when to write a letter to ask a question, participating in protest, or visiting legislators and other decision makers is as essential as is the need to be a registered voter. In order for that letter, protest, or visit to carry any weight with the person to whom it is addressed, constituents must be aware of the issue and concerned enough to act. Voting citizens' voices are heeded. Knowing the importance of the election process, the need to cast a vote, and the engagement to do so means our democracy will survive. As Sandra Day O'Connor said, "As a citizen, you need to know how to be part of it, how to express yourself—and not just by voting."[7] It is incumbent on educators to make sure that children become engaged, interested, and willing to work within their communities and their nation.

This book details the many opportunities schools and librarians have to cover these four areas as they relate to elementary, middle, junior high, and high school. Ideas are included for coteaching with colleagues in their classrooms by providing instruction and the many ways support can be given to students through library programming and activities. An underlying premise is that you will take a leadership role in making sure your students are given this information even if it is not taught in their regular classrooms.

When information literacy is taught independent of classroom assignments, it is difficult to give students opportunities to practice their research skills. If they are not taught real-life skills in their classrooms, there is no certainty that all students will be exposed to them since not all students experience the same possibilities in their lives. The real-life activities proposed are reinforced in the library throughout all grade levels so that any lesson missed at one level can be covered at the next level and in ways that make the learning applicable to them. Recognizing that you may have only volunteer help in managing your library or may be in more than one school, the implementation may seem impossible. This means careful planning to set attainable goals.

As an instructor, you can create your own Year Plan with a set of goals for your school year. No doubt it will change many times, but creating a plan for the year means you are thinking of what you would like students to know and understand about real life by the end of the year. You have some activities you might try, thinking about the outcomes of each one. While things may change and you may not change the end goal, you may need to take a different road to get there. Having the following template in an electronic spreadsheet will allow you not only to develop your Year Plan but also to add columns to record the success of your effort by noting participants and measures used. It should help you form your thoughts, create strategies, and record your trials. You can put them in order by priority remembering that it is your guide, not your directive. It may be that you can only implement one activity in one section each semester.

Reproducible 1-1

YEAR PLAN: REAL LIFE

Teaching Module: _____

Need	With*	How-To Activities	When and Time Needed	Anticipated Outcomes	Test for Success
Set Goals					
Create Plans					
Next Year					
Other					

Note: *(t)eachers, (g)uidance counselor, (a)dministration, (s)tudents, (p)arents, (c)ommunity.

What Can I Do: A Planning Document

These templates can be used at any level with the needs, persons equally responsible, activities, anticipated outcomes, and tests for success planned for the appropriate grade level.

In the Education Environment, I will be able to [*sample for grades 7–8*]

Need	With*	How-to Activities	When and Time Needed	Anticipated Outcomes	Test for Success
Set Goals	t, g, s	Library orientation	1st week of school	Students will review their course schedules.	
Create Plans	t, g	Library orientation	1st week of school	Students will review extracurricular activities.	Have students grouped to review choices for availability to implement choices; Plan B if choices overlap.
Next Year	t, g,	High school counselors and students	1st semester	Students will understand choosing classes.	Review student registration for high school courses.

Career Information will be provided to students [*sample for grades K–3*]

Need	With*	How-to Activities	When and Time Needed	Anticipated Outcomes	Test for Success
Identify Careers	T	Choosing careers	Semester with a review at a program for parents.	Students will research a career in depth.	Each student will have conducted one interview, constructed a picture of the workplace, and found information about requirements for job and salary and . . .
Requirements					
Salary					

(continued)

(continued)

My Economic Awareness activities will include [*example for grades 9–10*]

Need	With*	How-to Activities	When and Time Needed	Anticipated Outcomes	Tests for Success
Financial Literacy Lessons	t, c	Open a checking account.	Lunch hour	Students will understand banking.	Create a bulletin board for the library showing how to open a checking account, monthly costs of this, and cost of writing checks. Another bulletin board could show opening a savings account.
Cost of Training	t, g, s	Present how to find information about costs of training.	Lunch hour for one week	Students will create a database of info about colleges to share.	Number of students who attend.

Teaching Civic Responsibility will include [*example for grades 10–11*]

Need	With*	How-to Activities	When and Time Needed	Anticipated Outcomes	Tests for Success
Register to Vote	t	League of Women Voters speaker	November	Students will be given voter registration forms.	Number of 18-year-olds who actually register to vote.

*Note: *(t)eachers, (g)uidance counselor, (a)dministration, (s)tudents, (p)arents, (c)ommunity.*

Exercises, activities, field trips, and other events are suggested to help you plan. Some of the activities may seem repetitive, but while students start learning about community helpers in the early grades by identifying who they are, by the time your students are in high school, they have synthesized that knowledge and are now able to look at the many roles that these officers, government workers, or other roles offer to the citizens of their community. This will increase in depth of activity such as the elementary school election vote to the middle school students' ability to visit a lawmaker to the high school students perhaps supporting a candidate during an election. Each of these may seem to be proscribed for a level, but the activities can always be changed to meet the needs of the class at hand. For example, elementary school students could visit a lawmaker's office if they have been studying an issue that this legislator backed, or a study of the government. As you read through the activities for one level, many can be easily adapted to other grade levels, and some resources listed in one grade may also offer lessons or activity ideas for other grades, or similar or complementary topics.

Many of the suggested activities are tied to a curriculum that might already be in place. You can collaborate with teachers using this curriculum, and exercising your leadership skills, you can suggest ways that they can expand, further support, or provide resources. You can let students practice what they have learned in the library.

Further, one of your primary roles is to make sure the collection of resources is adequate to support all the teachers and to help every student. Frequent check-ins with grade-level or department chairs, district curriculum coordinators, and individual teachers bring many opportunities to begin discussions on further collaborations. Guidance counselors are major players in helping with both vocational information and those tests that students will face when choosing an occupation. They will also be essential to helping students choose where to go to learn more after high school, the institutions they want to enter and the qualifications and process for that admission, and how to obtain funding to carry out their continued education. Your collaboration with the counseling department can include not only the purchasing of resources but also the creation of class and schoolwide initiatives that cross grade levels and build upon each other.

Each grade level will build on the previous one. It is anticipated that parents and members of the community will be involved in many of these activities. There are many government and private financial institutions that support schools with "real-life" curriculum that can be accomplished in the classroom and/or library.

Content standards abound for all these areas of study. All of these—C3 Social Studies Framework, Next Generation Science Standards, Common Core, as well as National School Library Standards—ask students to think critically, ask questions, participate in their school and community, create new information, and share their ideas. Any of the activities listed in this book can fit into a well-planned standards-based lesson as part of any content area.

The concepts and activities described for one level may be introduced or reinforced earlier than presented. These underscore all activities:

- Asking question to create engaged, inquisitive, and active learning.
- Evaluating all information critically—the source, the perspectives, and the intent—is the backbone to understanding events, time, and people.

- Encouraging innovation and self-awareness through active, hands-on, and purposeful investigation that will build needed skills.

- Finding that discovery is personal but relies on community interaction and social engagement.

The chapters of this book offer the core concepts, activities, and resources arranged in ways that allow you to choose the lesson or activity and apply it in the way that makes sense for you, your class, and your lesson goals. While the chapters are divided into grade levels, the activities and lesson plans might better fit a lower or higher grade level in your school. The focus here is to start students through the process of preparing for a life after school. Sometimes that life begins earlier than graduating from grade 12. One premise behind the suggestions in this book is the knowledge that students who do not finish high school often face financial hardships that permeate other parts of their lives. The chances of finding traditional work diminish with each new technological advance. Therefore, you and all school librarians can, through each year, keep students focused on what is happening in their school at each grade level to provide all students with a better reason to remain in school, to help them see why what they are learning is essential to their getting their diploma and continuing to learn other skills. However, one must recognize that the public school system is not for everyone, and you can help with suggestions for other educational opportunities, including taking the General Equivalency Development (GED) test, higher education classes, internships, technical schools, home schooling, and the military.

This book acknowledges that, for some students and in some schools, this will be a greater challenge than in other schools. Underfunded public schools facing the choices of completing curriculum will wonder how to incorporate "yet another thing" into a crowded school day. Teachers face students who come to school each day without breakfast and go home after school to an empty house because their parent(s) may work at two or three jobs in order to survive. They may spend the evening with no dinner. It can seem difficult to convince these children that a future one might describe as the middle- or upper-class way of life will even be desirable, much less attainable. How much greater it is to help students adopt goals early as a part of what they can expect for themselves as adults. Short-term "enticements" in the forms of gangs, drugs, or other activities can be hard to ignore, but with guidance, support, and resources, you, leading and supporting collaboration with your teachers, can help create the system of expectation that all students can, indeed, graduate and follow their dreams.

The key to all this is to learn to like every student and convince each student that you can be trusted, that the information you help them find will address their need, be accurate, and if not helpful, that you are there to provide more information. You have to convince them that they will have your trust and that you hope they will trust you in return. The difference between telling students about opportunities will never be as acceptable as sharing with them what you trust will help them succeed. Obviously if your only chance is to give a talk in front of a class of 30 students, it will be no more helpful than an information literacy lesson where no assignment to conduct research and write a paper has been given. Anticipating and meeting needs begins with students and their needs, and they must trust you to find out what they are and help solve their problems.

Preparing students for the future begins the minute they enter a school building. Their proscribed classroom curriculum may cover much of the information in this book, but it is important that teaching is tied to the real world in such a way that students internalize what they are hearing, and it becomes sustained learning. This book outlines a process that builds from one level to the next grade, refreshing their past information and helping them build new knowledge at each step.

For the college-bound student who has known since birth that high school is only a first step, the path may be easier; for others, not so much. Academy Award, Emmy, and Tony winner Viola Davis spoke about it in New Orleans at the 2018 American Library Association conference. Her message came from her experience growing up in poverty. She explained that when people say to a child from a home like hers, "Work hard, make good grades, stay out of trouble, and you can do or be anything," that child is thinking, "Tell me how." This book "tells you how" to help that child as well as assist all children in planning their life after graduation from high school.

Notes

1. Amy Mitchell, Jeffrey Gottfried, Michael Barthel, and Elisa Shearer, "Pathways to News," Pew Research Center Journalism and Media, last modified July 7, 2016, accessed July 1, 2018, http://www.journalism.org/2016/07/07/pathways-to-news/.

2. Pew Research Center, "Social Media Fact Sheet," Pew Research Center Internet and Technology, last modified February 5, 2018, accessed July 1, 2018, http://www.pewinternet.org/fact-sheet/social-media/.

3. American Library Association, "Library Bill of Rights," Issues and Advocacy, accessed July 1, 2018, http://www.ala.org/advocacy/intfreedom/librarybill.

4. Michael Hansen, Elizabeth Levesque, Jon Valant, and Diana Quintero, *The 2018 Brown Center Report on American Education: How Well Are American Students Learning?* Brown Center on Education Policy at Brookings, June 2018, p. 2, accessed July 23, 2018, https://www.brookings.edu/multi-chapter-report/the-2018-brown-center-report-on-american-education/.

5. Emily Cardinali, "What Your State Is Doing to Beef Up Civics Education," July 21, 2018, p. 1, accessed July 24, 2018, https://www.npr.org/sections/ed/2018/07/21/624267576/what-your-state-is-doing-to-beef-up-civics-education.

6. Ibid., p. 4.

7. "Sandra Day O'Connor Quotes," BrainyQuote, last modified 2018, https://www.brainyquote.com/quotes/sandra_day_oconnor_471730.

Chapter 2

Beginning Early with Preschool, Kindergarten, and Grades 1–3

As students enter the doors into school for the very first time, they arrive from very different experiences. Many come to school with no preschool attendance, have little access to literacy activities, or have rarely traveled beyond their local neighborhood. Others come ready to jump right in, knowledgeable in the ways of preschool, day care, or other social-based experiences. Those without such a background may have problems learning to read because they have not had the exposure to rich language and other learning experiences. Helping these children "catch up" is a difficult challenge because it is hard to re-create a lifetime, short as it is, of literacy and experiential activities within the boundaries of a school year. Difficult? Yes, but not impossible. You and other school librarians are perfectly placed to create word-rich, experience-building environments for all students. Starting with connecting and collaborating with local libraries, you can continue with some of the initiatives and activities that their local libraries have created. Encouraging new-to-school parents to use their public library to gather up more reading materials can go a long way to encouraging lifelong library users. Remembering that some parents may feel that they do not read well enough to share reading with their children, you can help them discover the many programs available to parents at their libraries. They can also find activities there for themselves along with those for their children.

Most public library systems participate in some sort of early learning activities. Visit them yourself and see how you and they can help to bridge that world for these new school-going parents and children. Some Suggested Resources for Further Information, developed by children's librarians in public libraries for helping preschool children, are found at the end of the chapter.

Another dividing factor for young children entering school is that compelling computer, in the form of a laptop, tablet, computer, or phone. Many discussions cover when, if, why, or how these technologies should be introduced to children; however, the reality is that when going out to dinner or shopping, one sees that many parents have handed over their cell phones to children while waiting for the food to arrive or to keep them occupied while a purchase is completed.

No matter what one feels about this, some children enter school with a great deal of computer time behind them. For others, this happens not so much, whether by active decision making by parents or by lack of access. Regardless of how much screen time children have already had, they do seem to master very quickly those things they like doing online if they have access to a computer and the opportunity to experiment. It can be a challenging but effective way for children to learn and practice basic skills that will enhance their learning through play, and many school libraries offer software that is compelling as well as instructive.

If you are a librarian in a publicly funded school system that offers preschool, you are lucky and can begin to work with those teachers to help reinforce what they are teaching when students come to the library. Otherwise these experiences begin in kindergarten, and those children who have not been a part of preschool will rely on you to provide that extra boost toward experiences with print and media.

At this level, you can partner with your teachers to try to build the social-emotional development (SEL) that was missing in children from three to six. SEL is defined as a process where children "acquire and effectively apply the knowledge, attitudes, and skills necessary to understand and manage emotions, set and achieve positive goals, and feel and show empathy for others, establish and maintain positive relationships, and make responsible decisions."[1] These authors continue, "Children growing up in poverty are particularly likely to show delays in the social-emotional and self-regulation skills needed for school success, due in part to their heightened levels of stress."[2] A child who has been raised in a stressful environment, which may happen when this child lives in a low-income neighborhood whose primary caretaker is a single mother. These children have not been given the opportunity to learn how to pay attention, respond to questions, or handle frustration. To survive, they have learned to tune out of the situations going on around them, so their listening skills are very poor. "It is essential that kindergarten teachers, *librarians* [authors' insertion], and other early childhood educators understand and appreciate that these delays can result in disruptive classroom behavior that does not reflect conscious, willful disobedience on the part of the child."[3]

Responsibilities for the School Librarian

Your role with children who are lacking in SEL can be more than how you react to their behavior in the library; it may be enhanced by your collaboration with teachers to provide an oasis for students who need a quiet corner for a time-out period. You and your teachers will need to work with the school counselor to determine what can be done to help the child overcome the dynamics of the immediate trauma while making the library a tranquil option and not a punishment. In many cases this is not just misbehavior but also a function of past experiences at home. These students lack preschool experiences such as visits to the public library.

The public library children and youth librarians are major providers of experiences for preschool children when parents take their children to the library. The collaboration between school and public library can be a crucial bridge for all students, creating awareness that the public library is a place to go outside of school all through their K–12 years for storytime, fun activities, and homework help. Public youth librarians welcome your help to get information home with siblings, announcing storytimes and their other free early childhood experiences as well as programming on Saturdays and summers for all children. Inviting them in to your school to talk about their many programs for adults and children during an open house or back-to-school night can go a long way to building long-term collaborations and connections. It is very nice to have a colleague in the public library with whom you can bounce ideas as well as create fun school-to-community collaborations.

You can encourage your students in these grades to ask their parents and other caregivers to take their younger siblings to the library for storytimes and to check out books. You can suggest that students ask parents to help them get their own library cards so they can check out books from the public library as well as the school library. Remember that some parents might be reluctant to share their home addresses with an outside agency for many reasons. Some parents are not documented, while others may be hiding from an abusive situation; you can help these parents by encouraging them to make that first step because public libraries have many options for helping people gain access to all their services without identifying their status.

You are responsible for giving every student as much opportunity to become a good reader as possible, and this means getting as many books home with kindergarten and first-grade children as possible. Some of these students will have a parent or older sibling read a book to them in one night and need another for the next night. Others may not be fortunate enough to have someone at home to encourage reading. Setting up reading circles in your library where older students read to younger students is but one example of how to encourage reading for the youngest students.

Working with classroom teachers, you may be able to help connect older siblings who can take on the assignment to read to their sisters and brothers and to listen to these children read back to them. If the child is the oldest in the family or has no siblings, yet needs someone to read to or listen to, you can encourage him or her to ask parents or caregivers to suggest a neighbor who could spend 15 minutes with the student and a book. If your city has a mentoring program that connects volunteers to kids, suggest this service to the parents in your school. In some towns, local clubs and businesses might have volunteers read to elementary children or listen to students when they are learning to read. One of the book's authors well remembers her principal whose teachers sent struggling readers to his office to read to him when they had mastered a text. It gave the principal an opportunity to spend quality time with a student who was not in trouble, while encouraging these readers by sharing their success with an important adult in their lives. Have children copy the public libraries that often offer "dog listening" events at the library where children sit down in a comfy spot with a trained dog and read out loud to the dog. Suggest they read aloud to their pet or perhaps to a favorite stuffed toy.

Reading is essential in these grades, and you need to make sure your library has enough resources to make it possible for students to have access to them as easily and as often as possible. Providing adequate funds to buy books is the responsibility of the administrators who develop the school district budget. At other times the community may assist.

> Helen Snively, librarian at the Grand View Elementary School in Manhattan Beach, California, reports that her local Rotary Club donates funds for our elementary library programs to purchase books of their choosing. "Once a year they visit our K–2nd grade students during their library visit to read a story and talk a little bit about the importance of loving books, reading, libraries, and community service." She coordinates the event at our five elementary schools.

As students learn to read, they should take one or two books every night, and they should not have to wait even one week for their class to come to the library to exchange their books when the school library is their only source for outside reading. This involves a larger discussion about flexible scheduling as well as the number of books children are allowed to check out; however, school librarians are about access, and school libraries that remain open to all students throughout the school day and have no limits to numbers of books will create a school culture of reading. Working with your faculty and administrators to create this reading culture can go a long way to encouraging all students to carry a book with them at all times, knowing that they can always pull it out for a quick read. Welcoming students to the library before and after school and during the lunch hour can help this.

If this is not enough time, give teachers rotating classroom collections so they can encourage students to take away different books every night between their visits to the library.

To create classroom collections that "float" to classrooms for a month or six weeks or so is not difficult. This can be a cart of books, perhaps on a thematic topic of study, research books, or a wide variety of new-to-them books for in-class reading that is changed at least once a month. Those students who have discovered authors or books that they want to read again and again can do so when the books return to the library. Or they can head over to the library at lunch to get more. If you have problems with time to make the selections for the classroom collections, these can be "assigned" to students in the classroom. You will be surprised how carefully they make these selections and how well they know the likes and dislikes of their colleagues as well as their reading abilities.

You might also be able to find tutors in the local high schools to do some tutoring as a part of their service units. Check with the public librarian to see if the library's homework center has tutors who could accommodate beginning readers. Together, you and your classroom teachers can find many possibilities to allow any struggling student to have someone to help.

One of the joys of librarianship with young readers is creating the storytime or booktalk. The goal is to make books so appealing that students want to take the book away to read or listen to another time. Many of the books you choose will be new books in the library or fun books you have read before, while others may have a message that you want to convey: for example, the themes of this book, careers, understanding money and what it can buy, and how to become a good citizen. However, any titles you share with the entire class should be to encourage their reading on their own. Offering spots for "60-second" booktalks can bring students to the library to hear from peers what might be the next great book to read. Given only one minute to persuade potential readers to the joys of this recently read book can be challenging but quite fun for all. No plot is given, just a short, evocative presentation to convince others that the book is just right for them.

If your coursework in college did not focus on teaching reading, you are not expected to be a reading expert. Nevertheless, having more information about how to encourage children in your library to read will help you improve your skills. Some ideas for professional books to help you understand this are listed in the resources section at the end of the chapter. If you do not have a copy of any of these books, one of your teachers might own one. If not and your school district has a profession library, these titles may be available there; another option is to use your public library's interlibrary loan.

If your school has limited funds for technology, with few computers in classrooms, creating learning stations in the library for students who need to practice to improve skills will give that opportunity whenever it can be scheduled. Having teachers help select appropriate software allows you to make the best choices and also reminds teachers that there are resources in the library for students who need extra help. Asking for items from software vendors to preview brings those resources that have been reviewed and approved by others to your library, and setting a specific time for teachers to preview these new programs together allows discussion of their needs and demonstrates the role of the librarian as an active instruction partner there to help improve learning in the school.

One of the key goals of early schooling is to help students learn how to share with others and learn to work in a group. These are a part of classroom behavior that is required throughout their school years as well as into adult life. The work environment often includes working together in units to complete projects both face-to-face and online. Elementary students can begin to learn how to work with others to accomplish a goal. You begin this instruction informally and reinforce these experiences each time you place children in groups to share the books they read, or as they participate in your library activities. Many of the activities in this chapter provide assignments to do group research. Learning to work in a group begins here in early elementary school.

At all times, collaborating with teachers will enhance the curriculum and make you a recognized partner in teaching and learning. In many schools the school librarian is considered a "flex" teacher, and students are taken to the library while the teacher heads off for some planning time. While this is not a desired school library-classroom connection, beginning slowly you can make changes. You can use this time to teach the life skills of this book. Most likely, at some point early elementary curriculum includes "community helpers." You can introduce such topics as these: where do you live, how police officers work, what the mayor of our city does, and how do you think you can help make your school or city better?

This is a good time to begin that list of persons you can call upon to visit the classrooms and library to discuss their occupations, what they must learn to do that job, and answer any questions the students may ask. Such a list can be created electronically and updated each year. You will become the come-to person when teachers need an expert from the community.

You can directly instruct, beyond "library skills," and include those topics you love and may have no teacher to instruct: art history, cartooning, science, geography, or other fun topics that support students while meeting standards informally. This will allow your students to learn and practice skills they will need as they grow into members of their community.

If being the flex teacher is the pattern in your school, some of the activities suggested here work best to spread to and be joined by more than one classroom. While it can be difficult anticipating an activity to fit into the curriculum and involving all teachers at a single grade level, there are many compelling reasons to try. Creating that "culture of readers" and helping to develop a sense of community can set the stage for many of the lessons they will have in class, while creating a bond and sense of expectations that students and teachers will know and use. This will take some selling skills on your part. You will need to be aware of exactly how to fit this into what they are required to cover in their classrooms and exactly how it is related to something they are teaching on a given day within a given week. Teachers following a curriculum guide may not be at the same place as the teacher in the next room. Being aware of when teachers are covering a topic you can collaborate on to fit your teaching in the library to reinforce what is going on in the classroom and keeping up conversations about whole-grade lessons are the small steps you can take to start a new culture in your school. Trying to organize a successful multiroom collaboration might start with kindergarten.

Kindergarten is a good level to organize a joint activity because these teachers give less emphasis on paper-and-pencil tests. The art of the picture book will be an excellent beginning activity because it relates to adults who read the story when their attention is caught by a picture that begins to tell the story. Any successful collaboration you have with another teacher can be shared informally with your other teachers, and getting another teacher to work with you will encourage most of the others to begin these collaboration opportunities. As Abilock, Fontichiaro, and Harada in *Growing Schools*[4] suggest, some of the best collaborations come about because the school librarian worked with one class and then everyone else wanted to get in on the act.

If your school is totally focused on test scores, you may need to move forward with life lessons on your own. You will be opening a window to the "real world," taking you and your students beyond things not specifically assigned in the classroom curriculum but preparing them for lifelong living and learning. Each area—educational environment, career information, economic awareness, and civic responsibility—can become a part of your storytime, lesson practice, and out-of-class programming.

Education Environment

Librarians in most elementary schools work with teachers who teach in what is defined as a "self-contained classroom," a multidisciplinary classroom. Teachers are responsible for the entire curriculum for their single grade level. Anyone other than that teacher is considered to be a "special subjects" teacher. These specialists teach art, music, physical education, or other "additional" subjects. Others with a defined role include technology specialists, reading specialists, and instruction specialists. Should your school be missing any one of these "special subject" teachers, you can take responsibility for restoring some of these experiences through "real-life" or "cultural-literacy" experiences: helping students recognize the recreational and many cultural possibilities in their lives after high school.

While entertainment for children after school, on weekends, and on vacations hope-fully will be more than gaming or watching television, many students are indeed doing just that. If your school system has cut music, art, and physical education teachers from your staff, then the many students who do not have access to outside activities have no way of experiencing these things. You can collaborate with your teachers to fill in some of these missing experiences. It may mean enlisting the help of those special teachers at other levels in the school district or members of the community who can help you with ideas to share in the library. Asking the principal for time at a teachers' meeting to listen to a brief presentation can remind teachers of the need for music, art, and physical education in the adult world and offer time and space for planning these kinds of collaborations with teachers. You can start by finding how you might be able to fit this kind of learning into their teaching and if they have suggestions for people in the community to help, thus gaining their buy-in to those beginning steps toward longer teacher-librarian collaborations.

For some principals, these "special subjects" in their schools are, as mentioned earlier, their way to meet guidelines for a planning period for their teachers who then bring the stu-dents to the library and depart. This method of scheduling is not helpful in trying to plan collaborative teaching and learning, and it will mean you need to be very assertive in what appears to be a helpful suggestion if you are able to integrate what you are doing with what they are doing.

The Education Environment section in this chapter and the others explains how to help students prepare for the next grade level, remembering they are building experiences for life after school. It begins that first moment across the threshold to school, and you can serve as the catalyst to make sure this essential learning begins with the earliest time the child enters your library. The library is so often the connection between "real life" and the classroom. The "how to succeed in the school process" is not necessarily taught in the curriculum, and children may not understand what will be required as they move to the upper-elementary grades with a change in format from the single self-contained classroom to changing teachers for different subjects. You can help to prepare them for all the changes they will be making through literature, music, art, and other activities and by bringing in other specialists to help you in the library with some fun collaborations. You will be show-ing, by example, that many teachers will come into their lives throughout their time in school, and each one brings something new to learn and explore.

Another education change that occurs in these earliest grades is instruction in how to "do school." This includes learning how to sit still when necessary, line up, raise a hand to be recognized for speaking, and work well in groups. Library storytime, makerspace activ-ities, and other library activities are excellent venues for young students to learn how to learn, how to participate with others in the learning process, and how to behave in learning situations. While much of this is taught in the classroom, the library is where they can prac-tice with your support and guidance.

Career Information

Children look with wide eyes at the fire truck parked in the fire house as they drive by, thinking how much fun it would be to be in that truck with the lights flashing. They know that policemen and policewomen wear blue uniforms and doctors and dentists wear white coats. The person who delivers mail wears blue, and the UPS driver wears brown. However, what do children really understand about what these persons actually do and how they learn to do their jobs? Working with your teachers, you can expand what they are doing in the classroom to help students learn about community helpers. This can be a fun activity as well as a learning experience.

A neighbor whose four-year-old son loved the trash truck would always wait at the corner on "trash day" to wave to the driver. When asked what he wanted to be when he grew up, the child would say, "I want to be a trash dude. They only work one day a week!" He was certain that since the trash was picked up on Wednesdays, that was the only workday for the driver. If only that were true! Investigations through reading, visiting the trash dump, and interviewing trash collectors can help, through time, to discover the real schedule of the local trash collectors. This is an excellent example of asking this question: With technologies changing the work environment, how will work schedules change? How might this four-year-old learn more about this seemingly easy, although wrong, idea about this job, both in and out of school?

Making connections with only what someone observed leads to incomplete information, as the neighbor in the sidebar discovered. Because a person does not see what happens throughout a worker's day, children and adults make assumptions about that work. Because so many of the jobs elementary students might hope to have "when they grow up" are based on observation, you can collaborate in the effort to begin to provide a more complete picture of what different community workers do. If this information is only quickly covered in the classroom, you can expand that information by beginning to teach the research process. Reading books, both information or nonfiction and imagination or fiction, allows your young students to see that information gathering comes from many sources. If you follow one of the many community helpers through their day via a story or article, you can make a chart of the activities that are accomplished by that employee. If teachers teach "community helpers" as a more substantive instructional topic, you can provide informative support through literature, activities, speakers, and other lessons.

For kindergarten children, recognizing the people who work around them is an identification process where they recognize what they do for the community and what they wear while they are doing it. Especially compelling would be talking about "service" animals that work to help people who need the extra help that a trained animal can provide.

Learning how they are trained can lead to families taking in puppies for pretraining or piquing the imagination to other jobs working with animals.

In first grade, students can start their community-helper investigation by looking around their own school. They certainly know their teacher. But what about having students check one of those specialist teachers or the custodian? They can begin interviewing those who work in your school to find out what they do all day, how they learn how to do it, and what they like best about what they do. Depending upon the size of the school, it may mean small groups will work together on a single interviewee. Using the Right Question Institute's Question Formulation Technique (QFT), they will, as a class, develop questions and then within their group prioritize those questions to fit their interview situation. They will be interviewing those persons who are working in the school cafeteria, the custodian, art teacher, school nurse, principal, secretary, crossing guard, and school bus driver. Are there others who come in to help? Identifying just who works at your school can be an investigative activity that entails students observing those around them. Making lists of jobs and the people who occupy them teaches organization skills. Informal information literacy at work! Invite students to draw a picture of their person. In the second grade, students can do more in-depth interviews with these school workers or can interview their parents, guardians, or other important adults.

In second grade, students can begin working on more in-depth research assignments. They can begin to work in small groups to share what they have learned, develop the questions they need to answer, and begin to use both print and electronic information to find those answers. Caroline Romano, a K–2 librarian for the Wallenpaupack North Primary in Hawley, Pennsylvania, teaches her biography lessons as a supplement to her teachers' nine-week career unit.

As you move further afield from school to community, parents or guardians might work in neighboring cities or elsewhere. With this assignment, some discretion is needed when students are from homes where parents are not working or where a parent may not be comfortable being asked about his or her employment. Inviting parents in to the library to talk briefly about their jobs can be a fun activity. Have "stations" where parents can meet with small groups of students for a short time, and then the groups rotate; this can be a way to meet many adults in a short amount of time.

By third grade, students should be able to see if there are people in their community they might interview, such as members of their church, synagogue, temple, or mosque or any adults they work with in clubs, sports, scouts, or other activities. When they bring these interviews back to the library, help them conduct research on what others do in similar jobs in locations other than their school or community and even in other countries across the globe. For example, does a veterinarian in another country, or even in a different part of the United States, work with the same kinds of animals as one in your town? What about a trash collector? Sharing these differences through bulletin boards, videos, or other methods allows the information to filter down to all students.

If your school is located near businesses, fire stations, department stores, restaurants, or any place where people offer services, a walk to one of these can be a way to find out about the workplace. It will require meeting all the requirements of a field trip, but it can be with little expense if the location is within walking distance.

Few students choose a career at an early age, but many, like our "trash dude," are attracted to any number of careers on the basis of their own experiences in their neighborhoods or larger community or something they see on television. Our culture seems to insist that parents enroll their children in various after-school activities such as music, ballet, or ice-skating lessons or sports. Children in families who can do so are encouraged to try many things, and their families hopefully allow them to choose as time goes by. Some children find their niche early, while others find that their choices will change through their time in basic education. Many children and their parents, with stars in their eyes, hope that an early obsession with a particular sport or activity will lend itself to a college scholarship and/or lucrative career. With information about those choices comes the need to understand the reality of the competitive sport, art, music, computer, and drama, among other worlds, which brings an awareness of what it takes to "make it" in those worlds. Hopefully this does not begin actually in the early grades, but many adults believe that even third grade is not too young for some to "settle" in with an activity with which they can stay for the duration of their youth.

Economic Awareness

Economic awareness or financial literacy is based in learning all about mathematics and how to calculate, but these are not always taught with examples that match what students are experiencing in their daily lives at home. For many adults, including some elementary teachers, even simple arithmetic is considered very difficult. When a child hears an adult say, "I have trouble even balancing my checkbook," an aura of mystery and insurmountable difficulty makes this a dreaded subject. This, coupled with the homework drill of dull pages and pages of problems to add, subtract, multiply, and divide, reinforces the sense of unease in this curriculum area. You and your students can create some one-sentence questions that will place math in the center of a library question.

The advent of the small handheld calculator or a cell phone with calculating capabilities has removed the problem of a calculation by hand, only the need to know which action to apply. The answer for any group of numbers calculated on paper can be quickly checked for accuracy. Some practice is needed to look at results to see if the answer is logical.

Working with teachers with their arithmetic assignments, you can try to provide some real-life experiences in the library to build financial literacy.

Kindergarten and first-grade students are just beginning to understand addition and subtraction. Some children are still unsure of the meaning of numbers, and teaching strategies in the early grades can include helping students identify these core concepts. They may very well know the value of money if their parents have started giving them an allowance. If they buy their lunch at school, they need to know how to recognize the correct change.

If the school has a store where students can buy pencils and pens, this can be used as an example of the buying power of a given amount of money. Students who belong to organizations where they are asked to sell products can be used as an example of a real-life activity in their lives. Girl Scout cookie sales are a part of this. If you have a book fair every year in your library, you can help them understand how to buy books before the fair opens.

Students may think when summer approaches that it might be a good idea to have a lemonade stand to make money, but will it offer a profit or a loss? This also offers an opportunity to teach financial literacy. You could check Sarah Sparks's article[5] in *Education Week* for information about a project in Indiana that is promoting National Lemonade Day for additional information. Originally supported by an Indiana entrepreneur, Scott Jones, developer of a search engine, ChaCha, which made voice mail affordable, National Lemonade Day is designed to allow students to become entrepreneurs and develop their financial literacy.

Students in third grade have math skills to allow them to begin calculating how to save money for things they would like in their future. It is a good time to show how saving a dollar can grow over the rest of the time they are in school and helping pay tuition for any training after school. It grows from what they are learning about their future careers.

Civic Responsibility

In his book for preschoolers through grade 1, Dave Eggers asks, *What Can a Citizen Do?* (San Francisco, CA: Chronicle Books, 2018). The concept of changing laws is offered simplistically and will help children begin to understand how to right wrongs. It is an introduction to the civics instruction they will have later in their school careers. At this level students learn the important role of recognizing the meaning of bullying and learn how to respond when a member of their class is being bullied and what should be done. This is a part of the education in every classroom, and you can help reinforce these efforts by classroom teachers. It is a part of the responsibility of being a citizen.

Civics instruction teaches the rights and responsibilities of citizenship. Children are taught citizenship skills in preschool when they are given practice in getting along with others, when they learn how to behave in certain situations and begin to develop their leadership skills. It also means acknowledging the care of community property such as the books they find in their library and classroom.

A fun part of teaching about the library includes teaching students how to take care of the books they take home. Because these books belong to the school, it means that they belong to all the children in the school. For eons, librarians in schools have charged fines for those who do not return books on time, or limit current checkout if the student has a book at home he or she forgot to return. Librarians discuss this all the time, and while most have begun to discontinue charging fines, there are those who believe that it is a deterrent to forgetting. Check out the following discussions about fines and life lessons here:

- April Dawkins, "Overdue Fees: Barriers to Access in School Libraries," *Intellectual Freedom Blog*, Office for Intellectual Freedom of the American Library Association, October 12, 2017, https://www.oif.ala.og/oif/?p=10955.

- "Life Lessons @ Your Library," *Library Journal*, May 22, 2013, https://lj.libraryjournal.com/blogs/annoyedlibrarian/2013/05/22/life-lessons-your-library/.

One way to think about fines and book returns is to encourage book return on behalf of others in the school. Teaching respect for all the belongings of classmates because the library belongs to their classmates can be a part of developing a caring school culture. Teaching this responsibility is done without assessing penalties such as fines or restrictions from taking another book if a student leaves a book at home.

Just like learning how to be a part of a school community is a part of early education, civic responsibility can be demonstrated in the library by asking students to consider library "rules." It would be a good time to let the third graders start considering why and what should be the library rules. This may take a little courage on your part, but if they create the rules, they are more likely to be willing to follow them. This activity can be a regular part of library orientation for the third graders each year, giving these students ownership of their environment.

Students learn about their home, their school, their community, and their nation. Learning the Pledge of Allegiance and the national anthem are ways to begin incorporating the larger world into the classroom. These are symbols of our national pride and give a sense of what it means to be a citizen of the United States. With their classroom teachers, explanations of the words, the reasons for saying the pledge to the flag, why it is said, why one stands for the national anthem, and the meaning of those words can be discussed as often as needed. The music and art teacher can both be helpful in reinforcing this learning.

Some students in a classroom or their parents may have been born in a different country. If it is unclear what their legal status is, it is not mentioned. However, if students who interview their parents find their grandparents or great grandparents came here from another country and were once living under a different flag with a different national anthem, sharing this helps expand the concept of living in a global community.

Students need to begin to learn about the people in their lives who are responsible for governance, laws and, in the case of school board members, are responsible for their teachers and classrooms. Whenever possible, these are persons to be introduced to your students. Working with your principal and teachers, determine when it is appropriate to invite a government official to the school. As previously mentioned, you will need to maintain an up-to-date list of the potential speakers.

It is never too early to begin talking about the responsibility to vote in elections. This can be a gentle, fun introduction by carrying out the voting process. Books can be read during storytime with the very youngest and, as students mature, conversations can be held about state and national elections. If an elementary school is a polling place, that election process will be, literally, on their doorstep.

This chapter has covered our four areas—education environment, career information, economic awareness, and civic responsibility—as they relate to students from age 4, preschool, to grade 3, 9- or 10-year-olds. Some of the activities in the chapter can be repeated or expanded in the next three grades.

Suggested Activities

Responsibilities of the Librarian

1. Invite the children's librarian from the nearest public library to come to your school to share programs offered at the public library. You can reinforce the value of storytime, access to lots of reading materials that children can take home, and the many activities that they can do with their whole family. This person could be invited to the library during any open house where he or she could speak with parents about getting a library card for their child. Consider other activities that the two of you can share, including parent-education evenings with family activities to encourage reading or help them "share these wonderful books with your children," makerspace activities for parents and children trading off both venues, or special events such as writing letters together to first responders or military folks or raising money for a local charity.

2. **Where do I live?**

Elements of the Activity	Description of How the Elements Are Accomplished	School Librarian Will . . .
GOAL: By the end of this activity, students will know and understand:	What are important buildings in my town?	Locate and print individual images of local buildings such as the following: Police Station Library Parks Fire Station Art gallery Museum Hospital or clinic . . . And any other local place of importance.
SKILLS: To be gained through this activity	1. Ability to identify local buildings and what goes 2. Discussion etiquette	Hold discussion—showing the pictures, guessing what they are, and sharing about what the workers there do. Asking if anyone has been there.

BIG IDEA: How does this relate to "real life"?	Knowing about "place" and "location" will give students a sense of what their town looks like on a map.	Draw a simple map on the board with locations of the school and some or all of your buildings.
		    "Place" is where you are (I am at school) OR an identified space (even if you're not there).
		    "Location" is where you are relative to other places, for example, addresses and latitude.

MATERIALS: Needed to complete this activity	Images—computer and screen.	Show images printed from online sources or taken personally and printed or shown on whiteboard or screen. Technology to locate, print, and share, if online, images.
CONTACTS:	Who is needed to complete this project?	For this activity, students will interact with the librarian, who will lead the discussion on where these buildings are in town using Google Maps for the whole class to see and demonstrate how to identify what buildings exist and where.
Reflect and review	Further actions we can take? How did it go? What else do we need to know/do?	**FOLLOW-UP:** 1. Speakers from these buildings, perhaps a field trip. 2. Collaboration with the teacher to create inquiry project: What if we asked students and their parents to take their own pictures of interesting places when they go downtown? You may need to provide a simple camera for those without one. Place them on a community board in the library and label each one. Older grades can use these same images to create a city timeline of when each structure was built as part of a "get to know my city" project. *Source idea:* National Park Service (nps.gov)

3. Maintain a computer list and contact information of individuals who are willing to come to school to speak to children about their occupations and what they should plan to cover. Some suggestions for the list include the following:

People	Contact Info
Mayor and other city personnel, police fire water treatment, and garbage facilities	
Court system, including judges, lawyers, court recorder, and bailiff	
School board, other school personnel at the district level	
Chamber of Commerce	
Better Business Bureau	
Store owners, workers in department and grocery stores, restaurants, auto dealers, and computer-repair persons	
Home-repair persons, such as painters, plumbers, gardeners, and television repair	
Medical doctors, nurses, hospital personnel, urgent-care providers, dentists, dental assistants, and physical therapy	
Recreation providers, professional sports persons, movie-theater personnel, and parks	
Museum and music performers, artists and art galleries, and symphonies	

Note: Because speakers are not always prepared to speak to students, you will be prepared to make the connections not only to find speakers, programs, and artists but also to help them present a program that is active, meets the goals of the classroom, and provides the ability to assess learning. Some programs are classroom/library ready, while others are our neighbors who do interesting things that students might like to know more about. You can partner with the speaker to develop an activity that encourages students to use different viewpoints, use new tools, or critically think through a problem. Hand in hand with the classroom teacher, the outside speaker or program can efficiently work with you to create as much of a real-life experience as possible.

4. **Art of the picture book**

Kindergarten. Read, or for more than one class of students, project a Caldecott book (CDs of these books are available from Scholastic). Explain how the artist is supposed to make the words fit the picture. Then go through the picture book again and match the words to the illustrations with children helping. This covers several teaching areas. It involves counting if the picture has items in it to be counted and coloring if the raincoat is supposed to be red. It involves science and the weather, the seasons, and ecology. This activity can introduce students to basic reading skills while incorporating the large concepts of community, finance, or similar topics.

Other suggestions include the following:

Grades 2 and 3. These students can have the Caldecott guidelines reviewed simply and, placed in groups, match these to Caldecott winners and Caldecott Honor Books in your library to see which seems to be a better match to those rules. Since there is no right or wrong answer, it is a group decision and becomes a final discussion with the entire class.

Lesson Plan

The art of the picture book

Counting, shapes, colors

Opening doors to invite teacher-librarian collaboration

Elements of the Activity	Description of How the Elements Are Accomplished	School Librarian Will . . .
GOAL: By the end of this activity, students will know and understand:		1. Grades TK–KindergartenChoose several picture books with "concept" of colors, shapes, numbers, or other concept to be learned. If reading to more than one class, project a book on a screen from a CD or online source (such as those by Scholastic). Explain how the artist is supposed to make the words fit the picture. Then go through the picture book again and match the words to the illustrations. This covers several teaching areas. It involves counting if the picture has items in it to be counted. It involves colors if the raincoat is supposed to be red. It involves science and the weather if it has anything to do with seasons. Other suggestions include the following: 2. Art of the picture book for grade 2. 3. These students can have the Caldecott guidelines reviewed simply and, placed in groups, match these to Caldecott winners and Caldecott Honor Books in your library to see which seems to be a better match to those rules. Since there is no right or wrong and it is a group decision, it becomes a final discussion with the entire class.
SKILLS: To be gained through this activity		Counting, shape identification, color identification, or other concepts reviewed. Introduction to Caldecott awards. Understanding guidelines and how they work to define an idea, object, or goal.

(continued)

Elements of the Activity	Description of How the Elements Are Accomplished	School Librarian Will . . .
BIG IDEA: How does this relate to "real life"?		Mastering knowledge of shapes, colors, and numbers is important across all areas of life.
MATERIALS: Needed to complete this activity		Picture books, projector if desired/needed
CONTACTS:	Who is needed to complete this project?	Might we be able to do this with all kindergarten classes?
Reflect and review	Further actions we can take? How did it go? What else do we need to know/do?	FOLLOW-UP: 1. Suggest curricular ties with learning about money, identifying shapes and words on signs. 2. Coteaching inquiry project about rules, guidelines, and awards.

Careers

5. In kindergarten and grade 1, to chart what community helpers do all day, you can read Peggy Rathmann's *Office Buckle and Gloria* (New York: G. P. Putnam's Sons, 1995) and Arthur Yorinks's *Hey, Al* (New York: Farrar, Straus and Giroux); both are Caldecott winners, which leads from the previous activity. Ask students to name the persons in the community whom they consider helpers and how they are helpful. See if they have ideas of what these people do all day in their jobs. You help them by starting with people around the school and then going away from the school. It is good to start with hints, but they should be able to create a very long list in a very short time, even in kindergarten.

6. **Community helpers**

   Kindergarten. When the students come to the library, have picture books or mounted pictures of persons in various occupations ready for them to see. Assign them to work with another student. Have them ask one another what they want to be when they grow up and then report what their partner has said. Writing those choices on the board will help them see the spelling of each of these titles.

   Grades 1–2. Show the pictures you have for as many of their choices as you have found. Ask them why these persons wear what they have on. If these are people who go to an office, why do they wear a business suit? Do they wear protective clothing and why? It may come as a surprise that six-year-olds watch enough television to know why policemen and firemen wear protective clothing and why a football player wears a helmet. It is a good time to ask if they wear a helmet when they ride their skateboard or bicycle. You might ask the art teacher to have them draw a picture of what they will wear to work if they do what they think they would like to do.

Grade 3. Students are asked to find pictures of community helpers both in the United States and other countries to show the similarities and differences in their titles, their uniforms, and their cars or trucks they use on their jobs. They can find the title of the person in another country; for example, the policeman in England is called a Bobbie or a constable. It is an excellent way to begin to help children understand differences in cultures.

General. "When I grow up" career book. Over the course of several weeks, engage students with a variety of role-model careers in coloring-book format. Have them pick the occupations that interest them and compile it into a book that they can take home. Encourage them to think broadly and check designs for gender bias. Encourage all kinds of possibilities! Sign up for Pinterest (www.pinterest.com), because it will be so helpful finding outline drawing pages. Searching for "gender neutral careers for toddlers" brings a lovely array of possible career library ideas.

7. **Right Question Institute** (http://www.rightquestion.org/)

Librarians who learn to use the QFT have a strategy to place in a myriad of situations: parent evenings, student gatherings, and instructional design. Learning how to ask questions early and encouraging classroom teachers to use this process regularly as a part of larger inquiry processes will allow students to gain confidence not only in asking questions but also in knowing what the first steps are toward getting their questions answered. Even the youngest students can ask great questions and prioritize them according to the goal of their task. Using this QFT process, you can brainstorm questions that students want to ask about the job of the police. Their questions can often be used across all job sectors, but do not skip the opportunity to add in specialized questions for particular jobs. Using the QFT process from rightquestion.org can be accomplished by learning the process from their website or their book: *Make Just One Change*. This simple step-by-step process teaches students to brainstorm in a big way the questions that occur to them; then gives them a process for identifying them and prioritizing them; and, for our task of interviewing someone, lets them decide which question they want to know most about.

Sample questions to ask:

• When do you start work, and why do you need to begin then?

• How long do you work every day?

• What is your assignment? Here you may build upon related issues. The role of security guards allows the reinforcement of safety issues such as someone with a gun in the school.

- What are the people who work around you doing?

- Do you have to wear a special kind of clothing? Why?

8. Students will draw pictures of the persons they interview as well as their places of work. These will be on display in the library for parents' open house.

9. Caroline Romano's plans for a biography lesson for each of eight days includes the following:

For high-performing second-grade students and for third- and higher-grade students, reports like Caroline's and her teachers' are excellent fact-gathering reports that can be used as first steps in a longer inquiry into people and the work they do. Dividing the class into groups, using information each group found, they could create a timeline of where each individual biographee lived within an historical context. During that timeline, consider the ideas, inventions, and changes these people made and group them by area they impact, such as political, economic, cultural, or social. What in their lives made it possible for them to be the persons who have those ideas or inventions that made the change? Then ask each group to research those ideas and how they impact their lives today; how did their work benefit people today? For example, if a biographee was Jane Addams, an example of a community helper who does similar work might be a social worker.

Day 1

Beginning questions: If you were thinking about a job you could do when you grow up, how would you find out more? What research would you do? Look at career books? Tools used? Biographies? What is a biography? If a person is famous, why do we want to read about him or her? What can the person tell us about how he or she makes a difference? What is an autobiography? Would this be a way to start? Where would you find biographies in the library? What would you look up to find information online?

She reads a biography she is passionate about and then asks students to think about what he or she did to change things? How hard it was for this person to live his or her life? What did the person have to face? What was the person's job? In preparation for the next visit, she asks students to come in with an idea of whom they would like to research and why? She reminds them that, during their lives, their job could change more than once. It is good to get ideas.

Day 2

To prepare students for the assignment, she asks, Who has an idea of what they would like to study? She begins preparation for the assignment with "Today, we are going to practice restating what facts we find because we cannot copy and paste from the computer or copy word for word from the book. Who can tell us why we should not? What happens if we do? When we write or create something, the wording needs to come from us." She then passes out the color-coded handouts to assist with differentiated instruction and display the "helper words" such as "was born, in, onto." She has students choose a fact and then use the appropriate "helper word(s)" to express the fact as a sentence.

Day 3

Students repeat practice of rewriting facts with new biographical fact sheets. Those who are able to complete the task individually may do so, while those who need more assistance may work with the librarian. She gives each of them a separate sheet with this type of information to help them with this "restating facts" exercise:

Name: Florence Nightingale; Date of Birth: May 12, 1820; Birthplace: Florence, Italy; Parents: William and Fanny Nightingale

Name: Juliette Low; Date of Birth: October 31, 1860; Birthplace: Savannah, Georgia; Parents: William and Eleanor Gordon

Name: Martin Luther King Jr.; Date of Birth: January 15, 1929; Birthplace: Atlanta, Georgia; Parents: Martin Luther King and Alberta King

Name: Roberto Clemente; Date of Birth: August 18, 1934; Birthplace: Carolina, Puerto Rico; Parents: Melchor and Luisa Clemente

Day 4

Students complete an activity sheet for in-house books. Is it a biography? Is it an auto-biography? A sample of this lesson:

For each book title, write "AUTOBIOGRAPHY" if the book is an autobiography, or "BIOGRAPHY" if it is a biography.

Buttons for George Washington by Peter and Connie Roop _____
A Girl Named Helen Keller by Margo Lundell _____
Eve Bunting: Once Upon A Time by Eve Bunting _____
Martin's Big Words by Doreen Rappaport _____
Rachel Carson, Friend of Nature by Carol Greene _____
Juliette Low, Founder of the Girl Scouts by June Behrens _____
Gandhi by Demi _____
Babe Ruth by Norman L. Macht _____
The Great Houdini by Monica Kulling _____
Dr. Seuss, We Love You by Patricia Stone Martin _____
Jane Yolen: A Letter from Phoenix Farm by Jane Yolen _____

After this they should share what job they are interested in so that they may begin their research. Show them PebbleGo and remind them of how to look up books in Destiny (which they have done previously) and of the biographical profile they will complete on Day 5.

> Fun Facts
> Information Sources
> Biography
> Report
> Book Title:
> Author:
> Copyright Date:
> PebbleGo Date:
> By:

Day 5

Model how to write the biographical profile. Have students work in pairs as they use PebbleGo and the books to create profiles. This may need two days.

> **BIOGRAPHICAL PROFILE**
>
> *Subject's Name:*
> Why this person is important: _____
> How they helped the world: _____
> Why I chose this person: _____
> I was surprised to find out: _____

Day 6

Share "Biography Report": Model how to write in complete sentences. Students will work in pairs.

Day 7

Students will work toward completing the project.

Day 8

As students finish, they will share what they liked the most from what they learned.

10. Inviting parents to school to talk about where they work is not an original idea. Collaborating with teachers, a parent can talk to more than one class in the library.

The questions in Activity 7 are useful at this time. If you are in a school where parents who are working cannot come to school, it is a good time to ask someone from the community to come talk with students about their workplace. And as suggested earlier, the students in your school may have parents who are either not working or working at jobs they would not wish to share with the class. To add to this is to follow up with drawing activities so students can place their speaker into their work environment: for example, "Draw the laboratory that Sam's mother works in every day and place her there. What is she doing?"

11. With a teacher, plan a walk to a nearby business or community service. Discuss what happens in this location. If it is a restaurant, it may be the students have been there. Be sure to point out the people who work there that they may or may not see, because they work behind the counter or in the kitchen behind closed doors. Discuss why food from a restaurant has a cost associated with eating there. See the field trip handout.

Reproducible 2-1

FIELD TRIP!

When we can't go to the field . . . bring the field to the library!

Planning Tool

FAQs:

What is a "field trip"?

If students want to understand what goes on behind the scenes of a local business, but their class cannot go there . . . a "field trip" invites them in.

How is it different from inviting a speaker to the class?

It isn't much different at all. Speakers bring a huge value to a classroom, but our "field trip" encourages teachers and their speakers to go a step further and bring to the students an inquiry approach.

What do you mean "inquiry approach"?

When students are interested in something, they want to jump in and participate. Many times when speakers come to the library or classroom, students sit patiently while the speaker . . . well, "speaks." We'd like to invite speakers to come in with an activity in mind that encourages each student's participation: building, "making," inventing, drawing, or other activities that can bring the business to the classroom.

Inquiry asks a question—research answers it. In the case of field trips, research is the active participation that builds answers to that question.

What is the role of the librarian?

Because speakers are not always teachers, the librarian is perfectly placed to make the connections—find speakers, programs, artists, and so on and help them to develop a program that is active, meets the goals of the classroom, and provides the ability to assess learning. Some programs are classroom/library ready, while others are our neighbors who do interesting things that students might like to know more about. The librarian can partner with the speaker to develop an activity that encourages students to use different viewpoints, use new tools, or critically think through a problem. Hand in hand with the classroom teacher, the outside speaker or program can efficiently work with the librarian to create as much of a "real-life" experience as possible.

Reproducible 2-2

	Classroom Teacher Will . . .	School Librarian Will . . .
GOAL: *By the end of this activity, students will know and understand*		
SKILLS: *To be gained through this activity*		
"BIG IDEA": *How does this activity fit into the "real world"?*		
MATERIALS: *Needed to complete this activity*		
CONTACTS: *Who will be coming?*		
TIMELINE: *Suggestions:* 1. Meet to collaborate 2. Contact participants 3. Check in with admins 4. Collect materials 5. Publicity, if needed 6. Class preinstruction 7. Prepare the library 8. Greet participants 9. Enjoy! 10. Reflect and review	_____ _____ _____ _____ _____ _____ _____ _____ _____ _____	_____ _____ _____ _____ _____ _____ _____ _____ _____ _____

From *Teaching Life Skills in the School Library* by Blanche Woolls and Connie Hamner Williams. Santa Barbara, CA: Libraries Unlimited. Copyright © 2019.

Economic Awareness

12. Using library materials, play "library math." Here are some examples of one-sentence math problems you can solve in the library. Use student helpers to demonstrate instead of manipulatives.

    Adding and subtracting:

    • If you have three books to bring back to the library and you leave one at home, how many do you return? Give students three books and have them pick up two of them. How many are left?

    • If you have two library books in your desk, two at home in your bedroom, and one in your backpack, how many library books do you have?

    Multiplying and dividing:

    • Try this just before the class walks back to the classroom each week: Every student in the class now has a book. How many have been checked out today? What if everyone took out three books?

    • If only one-half of your room came to the library today, how many of your class would come to the library?

    Note: You could ask your students to expand this list for their class, and the third-grade students might write questions for the first- and second-grade students.

13. Brought to you by the Washington State Department of Finance, this online money-identification game with "Peter Pig" helps students identify the value of coins by asking them to identify the value and adding them up. This is excellent for the older students who are first learning how to identify denominations of money: https://practicalmoneyskills.com/play/peter_pigs_money_counter.

    ID the money, adapted from "money bags": http://www.teachhub.com/classroom-activities-teach-money-skills. Place paper bags with dollar amounts written on the bag on different tables. Let students work together in small groups to pick out cardboard money denominations from a central table that match the amount; for example, the bag with .25 would allow students to choose 25 pennies, 2 dimes and a nickel, 5 nickels, or other combinations. Place the money next to the bag and let other students check their matches.

    The U.S. Mint, https://www.usmint.gov/learn/kids, offers a wide variety of games and possibilities for learning about money. The link on collecting can help jump-start an interest in coin collecting.

    Start a coin-collecting club in the library.

    Invite a numismatic to your library to show off his or her collection!

14. Try this one at your next storytime. Frances Kennedy and Sheila Aldridge's book, *Pickle Patch Bathtub* (Berkeley, CA: Tricycle Press, 2004), tells the story of a young girl and her siblings who have outgrown their bathtub. It is in the middle of the 1920s and longer than before their grandparents were born. Life is hard without much money, and the children get together to save for a new bathtub. Based on a real story, this one makes for great reading.

    A wonderful follow-up is this lesson from the Vermont State Treasurer: http://secure2.vermonttreasurer.gov/legacywebsite/www.vermonttreasurer.gov/sites/treasurer/files/pdf/literacy/2012%20Kindergarten%20Pickle.pdf.

15. Plan a party and ask your students to help locate something to celebrate! Create a list of things to do at the party and a list of items needed. Create a handout or PowerPoint to list the costs of possible items so students can pick the items they want. Add up the total. Ask how they might pay for the party. If it is a gift from someone, let the class know the amount the donor gave and ask them to add up items and prices to that amount. Working together as a group, plan the party and then enjoy putting it on! Remind students that they are solving not only math problems but also "information problems." Start with their questions; QFT works well here with a Q-focus of "We want to have a party." Research the answers to their questions about what, where, when, how much, and what games, among others. This kind of activity demonstrates that research is something they will do every day to solve their information problems.

16. Girl Scout cookie sales are another time when the economics of the sales are a part of the student's life. Cookie orders are completed by parents, other relatives, their neighbors, and anyone they can get to make an order. While all the boxes have the same price, they have different flavors, and the exact numbers of boxes with each flavor are reported to the troop leader. When they are asked to sell at a local grocery store, they become responsible for instant sales.

17. With the art teacher, ask students to design book covers for a book they have read. This will reinforce the author's name and the title as information they need to find the book in the catalog. Place these "books" in learning stations with prices on sticky notes. Give students an amount of money they might spend in these bookstores and see how many books they would be able to buy with that amount. Teachers will need to work with you to make sure students have the math skills needed for setting the prices from 5 cents to 99 cents. Placing students in pairs for this exercise can have more able students helping others.

18. Before the school breaks for the summer, have students analyze how much they would need to sell a glass of lemonade to make a profit for their lemonade stand. They can match the cost of buying lemons and sugar to make lemonade and buying prepared lemonade. They need to remember all they will need, whether to serve in paper or

plastic cups or bring glasses from their house, where to find or make ice, and all the steps needed to carry out this plan. If you were able to do so, hold a class lemonade stand after school staffed by students over a two- to three-day period. The money earned could go toward a library book or to charity.

Civic Responsibility

19. Third graders, working in groups, could analyze those things in the library that need to be reviewed and perhaps changed such as how many books should be the number for a student to check out, for how long, and why do these need to be rules. With any rule, one needs to discuss the penalty for not following the rule and how or what is the outcome of imposing the penalty. These groups would need to list the pros and cons for any rule; for example, if students are allowed to check out 20 books, how does that affect the numbers of books available in the library for other students in the school to choose?

One way to create buy-in to rules is to have the students create them using QFT described in Activity 7. Students respond to the Q-focus: "The library needs rules." They ask questions about that statement. What may come up are some variations of these: "Why does the library need rules?" "What kind of rules do we need?" "What if we had a rule about being quiet?" "When do we need rules?" and so on. You write down their questions, and when all the questions have been listed, prioritize them and then pick out the questions that the students then discuss. They answer the questions while you write down answers, for example, "Why does the library need rules?" "Because it gets too noisy and I can't think," or "Because all the books would disappear." You might send students home to think about these questions or have students prioritize the top-priority questions to write on the board or post on the wall and let students think about them. Do this with as many classes as appropriate. The following week complete the project. This can also be completed during the lunch hour by asking students to pick out the top five answers. Highlight them. Ask students to put these answers into rules that might be useful: "When we walk into the library, we will speak in soft voices," "We will return our books on time," among others. Post those rules, probably no more than five, on a big piece of butcher paper and have every student sign it; keep it posted all year to point to when needed. Discuss why it might be more fun to post rules that are positively written versus those that are negatively written.

This process can also be completed on a number of topics such as rules for communicating online, which is one that is especially effective with students who begin to text as soon as they can "write." Create a similar butcher-paper sign with all the chosen rules and ask each student to sign it. One fun Q-focus idea is to use "the grandma rule." Students will find out that the grandma rule is one in which what they post online "will be all right for grandma to see." This meets civic responsibility standards on all fronts.

20. Patriotism includes the Pledge of Allegiance, our national anthem, and patriotic music.

    • Discuss the many reasons why "The Star-Spangled Banner" is performed at events and why the audience stands at this time.

    • With the music teacher, work to plan a program to share other patriotic songs, such as "America the Beautiful."

    • Read aloud from any of the many books about "The Star-Spangled Banner." Here are two to check out:

    Lambert, Nancy. *The Star-Spangled Banner*. New York: Penguin (Smithsonian), 2016.

    Spier, Peter. *The Star-Spangled Banner*. New York: Doubleday, 1973.

    Then use the directions from the Housing a Forest site—http://www.housingaforest.com/simple-american-flag-craft-for-kids/—to make an American flag. Play patriotic songs in the background. Youtube.com offers many varieties of video/music that can be played.

21. Do any students have parents or grandparents, or did they themselves come from other countries? What is the name of the country in the native language, and does that country have the same name that it had when they lived there? If you have a large size map, you can post locations with sticky notes and names, showing the diversity in your class. What does the flag look like? Ask them about their national anthem. YouTube offers many versions of national anthems, if students want you to play it. If they are willing to sing the words, students will be better able to understand what it means to "listen" to others in a global society. You can catch "World Cup" and Olympics fever with the National Anthem Channel that plays the winning anthems from across the globe: https://www.youtube.com/user/NationalAnthemsChan.

22. Ask students in your school to "name" your copy machine or other equipment. Read the book *Vote for Me*, citation given later, to explain the voting process. Begin by asking for names by having students place their ideas into a big jar. A week later, pull out the names and list them on the board or in the hall. If you like, give students time to advocate for their chosen name. On voting day, put out a big ballot box and have students choose their favorite. Use a group of students to count the ballots and make the announcement. The next week, proudly place the nameplate on the chosen piece of equipment.

    Other web resources are available from https://www.kshs.org/teachers/professional/pdfs/bruening_whos_boss.pdf

    You may adapt library activities for your state, town, and school from this fabulous lesson.

Books to read also include the following:

Bruel, Nick. *Bad Kitty for President*. New York: Square Fish, 2012.

Christiansen, Candace. *The Mitten Tree*. Golden, CO: Fulcrum Publishing, 2009.

Clanton, Ben. *Vote for Me!* Toronto, Canada: Kids Can Press, 2012.

Cronin, Doreen. *Duck for President* (A Click-Clack Book). New York: Atheneum Books, 2004.

Suggested Resources for Further Information

For help with teaching basics, go to www.ala.org/alsc/publications-resources/white-papers/importance-play and note the importance of play that you can use in your library. The Association for Library Service to Children (ALSC) website has two other white papers on this topic for additional information. Joining Betsy Diamant-Cohen's award-winning website, Mother Goose on the Loose: https://www.mgol.net/, can add activities and books to your programming for preschool and grade 1.

The first five years are detailed on http://www.first5california.com/learning-center.aspx?lang=en&id=11.

You can use some of the activities listed on this site with your youngest students. Think about using the "guessing game" at http://www.first5california.com/activity-center.aspx?id=18&sub=81) by creating several "grab bag centers" for students to wander to in the library and guess what is inside. Vary them over the course of several weeks so that as they walk in for storytime, they can only feel inside, with no peeking, and hold on to their guess until they reach the carpet. Then you can bring up the bag to the front, and the guesses can be shouted out, or teach raising hands. Pull out the item, and all clap their hands for knowing the answer. This can be an excellent part of a "coming to the library" procedure.

The Maryland Radio Network at http://wypr.org/programs/first-five-years brings a host of audio discussions on topics of interest to parents of young children. Librarians at schools with preschool and first-grade children can host their own parent night and bring a panel of local experts together to tackle one or more of these themes. Creating a regular monthly meeting can engage parents early on and help them create a bond with the school that their children will attend for the next several years.

The following is a list of suggested books on reading for you and your students' parents:

Barco, Kathy, and Melanie Borski-Howard. *Storytime and Beyond: Having Fun with Early Literacy*. Santa Barbara, CA: Libraries Unlimited, 2018.

Carroll, Joyce Armstrong, Kelley Barger, Karla James, and Kristy Hill. *Guided by Meaning in Primary Literacy: Libraries, Reading, Writing, and Learning.* Santa Barbara, CA: Libraries Unlimited, 2016.

Court, Joy. *Read to Succeed: Strategies to Engage Children and Young People in Reading for Pleasure.* London: Facet Publishing, 2011.

Court, Joy. *Reading by Right: Successful Strategies to Ensure Every Child Can Read to Success.* London: Facet Publishing, 2017.

Deskins, Liz, and Christina H. Dorr. *Linking Picture Books to National Content Standards: 200+ Lives to Explore.* Santa Barbara, CA: Libraries Unlimited, 2015.

Gooch, C. Kay, and Charlotte Massey: *Camp Summer Read: How to Create Your Own Summer Reading Camp.* Santa Barbara, CA: Libraries Unlimited, 2010.

Hobbs, Nancy, Kristen Sacco, and Myra R. Oleynik. *Personalized Reading: It's a Piece of PIE.* Santa Barbara, CA: Libraries Unlimited, 2010.

Krashen, Stephen. *Free Voluntary Reading.* Santa Barbara, CA: Libraries Unlimited, 2011.

Krashen, Stephen. *The Power of Reading: Insights from the Research*, 2nd ed. Westport, CT: Libraries Unlimited, 2004.

Krashen, Stephen, Sy-Ying Lee, and Christy Lio. *Comprehensive and Compelling: The Causes and Effects of Free Voluntary Reading.* Santa Barbara, CA: Libraries Unlimited, 2018.

McNeil, Heather. *Read, Rhyme, and Romp: Early Literacy Skills and Activities for Librarians, Teachers, and Parents.* Santa Barbara, CA: Libraries Unlimited, 2012.

Ross, Catherine Sheldrick, Lynne (E. F.) McKechnie, and Paulette M. Rothbauer. *Reading Still Matters: What the Research Reveals about Reading, Libraries, and Community.* Santa Barbara, CA: Libraries Unlimited, 2018.

Rothstein, Dan, and Luz Santana. *Make Just One Change: Teach Students to Ask Their Own Questions.* Cambridge, MA: Harvard Education Press, 2011.

Willingham, Daniel T. *Raising Kids Who Read: What Parents and Teachers Can Do.* San Francisco, CA: Jossey-Bass, 2015.

Wink, Joan. *The Power of Story.* Santa Barbara, CA: Libraries Unlimited, 2018.

Notes

1. Karen Bierman, Mark Greenberg, and Rachel Abenavoli. *Promoting Social and Emotional Learning in Preschool—Programs and Practices That Work* (State College, PA: Pennsylvania State University, Edna Bennett Pierce Prevention Research Center, 2017), 1.

2. Ibid., 4.

3. Donald A. Barr. "When Trauma Hinders Learning," *Phi Delta Kappan* 99 (March 2018): 44.

4. Debbie Abilock, Kristin Fontichiaro, and Violet H. Harada, eds. *Growing Schools: Librarians as Professional Developers* (Santa Barbara, CA: Libraries Unlimited, 2012).

5. Sarah D. Sparks. "How the Humble Lemonade Stand Is Becoming a Pipeline for Young Entrepreneurs," *Education Week*, July 29, 2018.

Chapter 3

Expanding Those Beginning Lessons: Moving Forward in the Middle Grades, 4–6

Not quite teenagers and no longer "little," these middle-grade students offer their own variety of wonderfulness. Still willing to participate in most classroom activities, these young tweens want to be a part of the larger world, *now*. Social media is compelling to these young people, and parents, concerned about their exposure, sometimes feel the need to curb cell phone activity. It is often hard to "peel it away" from them even at the dinner table since it appears they would rather be on the phone than concentrate on eating a meal. Medical professionals are worried about the impact of the cell phone on the health of those who have it to their ear, in their pockets, or in their hands 24/7, but it is indeed a part of our lives, and this age is an excellent place to continue or, in some cases, to begin instructing on polite phone habits.

Students begin to exercise their independence from their parents and other adults, becoming more reliant on social media, even texting friends who may be sitting in the next seat on the school bus. However, social media, in all its many incarnations, is here to stay, and rather than try to halt usage, opening the doors to what constitutes ethical and safe use of social media brings far better results and introduces a far wider discussion about safety, bullying, and information literacy.

Parents who are hoping their children will remain interested in learning a musical instrument or continuing dance lessons or tae kwon do may be dismayed when their children begin to be less interested in parent-generated activities and more interested in what their classmates are doing. With their friends in tow, they may suggest alternative activities for spending time outside of school.

Responsibilities for the School Librarian

Now that these students are in the fourth grade, they are better prepared with basic skills and are able to conduct research on their own, a skill that will grow over the next three years. Most students will have mastered the concept of alphabetical order and are experienced at finding answers asking questions on their cell phones. Their reading and comprehension skills are at a level where they can find more information in their searches and better understand the content because they have more life experiences to base their new knowledge. The challenges here come with the amount of information that students can locate because it is easy to get lost in the flood of information. Creating pertinent search terms to gain the most relevant information is an area of need at this stage, generating another important skill need: evaluating the quality, usefulness, and authority of the information that they do find. They need to learn how to select the most from their search. This is also a perfect time to spend time talking about passwords and online privacy.

In the first three grades, the school librarian helped push the development of reading skills and love for reading by reading stories, acting out stories, and encouraging writing stories and other reading-based activities as a regular part of library visits. Teachers at this level want students to be learning and using information-literacy skills. It becomes a constantly increasing challenge to make sure the skills you teach are directly related to a classroom assignment. This need for collaboration between you and the classroom teachers should encourage students to exercise their research skills often enough that they do not need to relearn them each year or even each semester. Information-literacy skills build upon the skills learned the prior year, and this kind of repetition of those beginning skills is reinforced so often that they become second nature. If you are in a school where teachers have not been including the resources found in the library in their planning process, it may take diligence and creativity to gain their interest and willingness to share learning experiences between the classroom and library. Building the trust that collaboration will result in a better learning situation comes about from small successful instruction activities, so do not be afraid to take a small step; it can then work into larger projects across multiple grades.

One approach is to talk with one or more teachers at the same grade level to show how you can add to one unit of instruction encouraging a wide array of sources for students to include in their research. Examples of collaborative library research topics are given in the book *Collaborative Research Projects*, by John D. Volkman, who recommends a stations approach for teaching searching skills. While the examples in his book are for grades 7–12, this method expands student research into listening to music or oral histories, viewing events posted on the Internet, and capturing pictures and other information. Learning stations encourage students to work together, learning how the dynamics of group work creates successful outcomes and are excellent activities that can be accomplished during "library time" in the elementary school. You can move learning stations into group exercises to help students learn to work in groups.

Volkman encourages sharing books and articles with other students; this allows students to bring their own experiences and observations to the group, which adds those individual strengths to help complete the group task. In creating learning centers, you are making judgments for accuracy of resources you want students to use. Your expertise in locating and evaluating resources will be an excellent addition to your teacher-librarian collaboration. You collaborate with your teaching partner, helping create assignments to teach students note taking and identifying useful facts, how to sort carefully through information, and eliminating bias and inaccuracies, the basics of information literacy.

Information literacy includes true examples of real-life skills students will use every day, but they are not all you need to make sure students learn and practice. Choosing which movie to watch, which party to attend, and how to get their homework completed before the next soccer practice is solved by identifying an information need, deciding what to do, and then completing the task. Adding to that, finding an answer—with the increase in the information that can be found—means you are well placed to help students recognize how to read, analyze, and write using their own thoughts and words when it appears to be much easier to cut and paste from the text found online. It is the time to begin discussions about fact-checking of information found in all sources. You can also begin to help students question the source of their information.

At the point where many teachers begin teaching research skills, many school librarians come up against the standard research assignment where students locate proscribed information about a state, animal, or other similar topic. While part of this process is designed to teach writing, organization, and information gathering, what often happens is that students use cut and paste to move information from the website to their paper. Librarians can encourage research-project shifts with teachers by introducing inquiry projects, but when this is not successful, providing students with programming that teaches the skills of information literacy can be a big part of your program. This can also use learning stations with computers or mobile devices. Students still must write their research papers so that their reports use good sentence construction and good grammar, and at these stations, students can practice using the spellchecker, formatting, creating tables, and other basic skills needed to make writing easier and more productive.

Even if you are not a part of writing projects, you can still encourage students with writing as a part of your agenda. Writing thank-you notes is an easy way to encourage students to write. In the past, what was a laborious task requiring good penmanship has now become a quick trip to the computer to create the text. Many can be e-mailed directly to the recipient. Sending thank-you letters to firefighters, military, or other community helpers and sending cheery letters to seniors in nursing homes are out-of-class activities that combine the best of information literacy and civics. You can collect them and send them as a group, keeping the recipients' addresses private so that students do not send multiple letters to the same author at the same time. Many authors of children's books try to answer every letter they receive, and with your reducing that number from 30 to 1 for the class, they are more likely to respond because it takes less time from their writing or illustrating.

Teachers responsible for drama and music will have performances, and students, whether in the performance or not, should be encouraged to invite their parents to the performance. Parents who attend should receive a thank-you note for taking the time to come. If an author or another visitor you have invited to the school for a program has come, the students can write the thank-you notes. You might be able to help students when parents ask them to send thank-you notes to relatives and others for gifts at birthdays and holidays.

Students need to learn how to write persuasive letters to persons they wish to influence. At this level, it could be a request to their parents for something they very much would like to have. The need to make careful choices of words that will be compelling to the reader will be an excellent introduction to how to convince anyone something is worthy of happening and how to persuade others to accede to the request. Calculating the cost of their request is discussed under Economic Awareness.

During the sixth grade, you may help the guidance counselor explain the differences between elementary classes and junior high school. Students in these grades have most likely remained in self-contained classrooms, and the change to multiple teachers will be very different. Another change is the actual size of the school. Most junior high schools will serve students from multiple elementary schools. The facility is larger, and the special areas such as the library, the gym, an auditorium, and the cafeteria are considerably larger. Students may be separated from friends in their sixth grade and need to make new friends. In some larger districts, performance groups for band and chorus may move students out of the building for citywide concerts, and sports teams also become competitive among the schools in the district. Movement into the next level can make the most outgoing and assertive student suddenly shy and the already-shy student withdraw into a cocoon.

Education Environment

Although some elementary schools maintain the self-contained classroom for these grades, in other school districts, students may begin to move from one classroom to another to meet with different teachers for math, reading, social studies, and science. Students begin to analyze their teaching styles and the degree of acceptability of different behavior patterns; they then can decide how to match their learning and behavior to these different styles. They will also be assessing your teaching style and the behavior you hope to maintain in the library.

The move from a single teacher to several is a big first step into the adult world. If it happens before the seventh grade, it means more than changing classrooms and teachers; it means being responsible to get all your belongings with you. Student backpacks are larger to carry their textbooks when they are not in the same room at the same desk all day. If they have lockers, the time to get to their lockers between classes may be short, causing them to come to your library with their library books still in the locker. They may be reluctant to take many additional resources home from the library because of the size of that backpack and the amount of homework assigned.

It is a time, too, when students begin to add outside activities that command their time and energy. They would like to make many decisions rather than waiting to be told or expected to adhere to rules that may seem meaningless to them. As mentioned before, this can cause tension at home when parents want their children to continue with activities that they have done before and the "tweens" are getting ready to flex some independence. You can suggest information for parents who are interested in online safety, perhaps offering speakers during parent nights to talk about this and other concerns.

Students will need much practice in communication skills to be able to respond to the variety of expectations, including making new friends. Helping students learn how to meet and greet newcomers is a quick etiquette lesson. A reminder at the close of this lesson is the need to write thank-you notes to thank someone if they have been treated to a ball game, circus, or other fun experience.

Their assignments from teachers will begin to require longer responses with the need, as discussed earlier, to explain how to get around the "cut and paste" of content and the need for accurate citations. Enhancing the information-literacy skills previously taught at each grade level is critical, and working collaboratively with teachers to ensure this continues to be a high priority. It is certainly time to implement the "inquire" standard to make sure all the students are reading, willing, and able to "build new knowledge by inquiring, thinking critically, identifying problems and developing strategies for solving problems."[1] At this age, students can be introduced to working in groups.

Working with groups, students learn that everyone carries a part of the load; learning that you can allow them to practice with the skills you teach, especially when the focus in their classrooms is on test results. Teaching to the test is focused on individual learning, and that approach limits the learning and sharing information that comes with working in groups. Your activities in the library can focus on creating group work that accomplishes many needed tasks.

Working with teachers and the guidance counselor, you can support preparation for the next grade-level change in classroom formats, and with the sixth-grade students, perhaps an actual visit can be arranged to the junior high school building. If this is not practical, create a virtual tour for grade 6. It would be a good time to invite the junior high guidance counselor to visit the school to introduce students to this next level.

Career Information

At this level, students begin a more serious approach to their choice of a career path. They need to understand the skills needed to apply for any position. Students start their awareness of the place of jobs in their lives and the salaries commanded for each. Learning which jobs are for people who want to work a regular schedule such as a department store and which may require different schedules such as a person who lives part of the time in the firehouse to be there when a fire breaks out in a building. Others may have jobs that require them to travel, such as pilots and flight attendants. Teachers may have an extended time off during the summer as well as school vacation times. For each occupation, students discuss educational requirements for the jobs that interest them, and discussions should include ways to save money for the necessary schooling beyond high school, whether it is college, trade school, or apprenticeship. The probable income for each of these professions is another factor in choosing a profession. Calculations for earnings and a little about the cost of training can be projects created and assigned by the math teacher; giving that subject a real-life view will be discussed under Economic Awareness.

Students may be moving on from what they considered their earlier choice, thinking they might like to become a firefighter, nurse, or a doctor because those are the occupations with which they are the most familiar in the lower grades. As students mature, they will become familiar with the wide variety of opportunities in the work force. Again, students can work in groups to research all those opportunities for work after high school.

Particular attention is needed for those students in schools where many come from homes with little or no income. These students are usually aware that they do not live as well as others. When they come from single-family homes and live in low-rent housing, or where there is considerable gang influence, these students have tough decisions to make. Even though it may seem futile to many teachers in these schools, you, your counselors, teachers, and community members can work together to find alternatives to help students break the poverty cycle they face. Gaining the trust of students when they may be in the school for only a short time is challenging, but this is essential for you to master. Recognizing you have answers and offer help, quietly, keeping their requests private can build trust very quickly, and these students in particular need to see how they can overcome their lifestyle pattern because you can help them start planning now. Libraries of all kinds have offered students "safe haven" before and after school. You can offer one-on-one or small group interactions, learning stations, makerspaces, and other activities to help them, even if they have only a short time with you.

All students recognize the need for financial security. Many have seen what happens when the business, factory, or department store where their parent is employed closes. They can begin to think about alternative professions that might appeal when one occupation is no longer viable. You can introduce students to the idea that they can transfer skills, that they can be more resilient if they learn more skills in school. They will prepare for today's work force that is changing very rapidly, but if they are prepared and confident, then they can fit their skills into the changing environment. Discussing the ability to return to education to obtain more job skills, a degree or certificate, can also help to show that as things change, they too can make those changes.

Activities in the library can help students continue their practice of interviewing by planning to meet workers in commercial ventures at the local level such as grocery stores, the nearest mall, agencies, restaurants, medical facilities, and factories. Many jobs are "hidden" from the casual viewer. In the grocery store, for example, there are many job roles such as the butcher or the baker who are seldom seen, while the person restocking the shelves, behind the deli counter, and checking out patrons is obvious. Technology changes are obvious in grocery stores that have patrons check out their own purchases. Other locations could be the local insurance agency? How do workers in a restaurant compare to fast-food venues?

Perhaps more difficult to interview are those persons who work in a hospital unless they live in the neighborhood. Roles in manufacturing may be researched, starting with the owner and manager of the facility and all those in the offices to the machinists and technicians who take care of equipment to the workers who remain on the assembly lines to produce products and those who load the trucks to take the merchandise away, and the drivers who must take special training to drive a semi.

From service and manufacturing careers, one can move to exploring transportation from bus drivers to railroad personnel, and then everyone who works at an airport, from those unseen in the control tower to those who check baggage at the curb, the airline ticket staff, Transportation Security Administration (TSA) workers, and the staff in shops and restaurants inside the TSA-controlled area. Lastly a move to careers in government, the local level, the license bureau, city hall's clerks and officials, the post office, to state government and then nationally in Congress and the White House, at the treasury and the mints, the presidential libraries, and the national and state museums. Such discussion will open interest in the kinds of jobs the government seeks. This includes those who assist elected government officials as aides in their offices and as persons who work on elections. This discussion helps set the stage for the later analysis of civic responsibility.

When these interviews are completed and recorded, they are shared with the class using a variety of methods. Library time can include discussions that cover which roles might be available to them while they are in high school and the impact of technology on these jobs. As students move through the grades, they can begin to refine their interests into career groups and continue searching for information.

Beginning the discussion of education needed for jobs can initiate thinking about what may be available for students to pursue in high school that will prepare them for a job immediately after they graduate. This can also be the beginning of a discussion of how finances impact decisions made after high school. Part of this is helping students simply recognize that there are apprenticeships, trade schools, community colleges, and four-year institutions, some of which will be accessible through online learning. If yours is a school where older siblings are likely to be in college or other learning institution, then this will not seem foreign.

Fostering a sense of relationship with an institution of higher learning helps to normalize the possibility that this could be an option. Any student who has parents or others who watch college football and basketball will recognize the team names, their mascots, school colors, and sometimes a few shots of campus life. These can lead to an introduction of campus life. You can use sports activities as a way to help generate information about these teams, colleges, and their locations. During March Madness, or the other college sport events, highlight the colleges, their songs, their mascots, and their many learning options.

Students may have visited college campuses. If so, they may be able to share why they were there and what they did while they were there. Did they see a dormitory room or visit a fraternity or sorority? Did they attend a sports event, and do they have a banner?

If you have a local campus of any kind, vocational, two-year, or four-year in your town, or nearby, you and the guidance counselor can organize a visit there to introduce your students to education after high school. The campus admissions office will be happy to have the opportunity to "sell" the campus experience and can talk about financial assistance available for tuition and other expenses. It helps raise economic awareness. Make some inquiries on what services they may offer to young people such as summer institutes, short-term classes, and other community-based outreach. You can become the campus liaison for this kind of information and advertise these events to students and faculty and parents. ▱

Economic Awareness

Math class can be a great time to collaborate in the classroom, or if your students have teachers assigned exclusively to teach math, ask them to participate in your effort to raise the financial-literacy levels of all students in these grades. They should be able to suggest ways for students to put their math lessons to practice in the library's financial-literacy lessons. You could go into math classes to talk about new books and other resources, and while doing so, explain the difference between prices of formats of books for the library and the cost difference and longevity of e-books, hardbound, and reinforced bindings. If you work with the teacher ahead of time, it is possible to develop some other library-related math problems. It is an opportunity to have a class help you choose some books by giving them a budget to work with making their selections.

Financial literacy has some realities that students may not have considered. They will know that if they lose their lunch money, they may not have lunch that day, but they will have even greater challenges as adults. The Federal Depository Insurance Corporation's (FDIC) *Money Smart* program for middle grades will help you teach this. ▱

Even if they may have suspected it well before now, students at this level learn that the tooth fairy is not real, just as they also realize that parents and others in their lives are responsible for the presents they receive for holidays. Previously, writing a persuasive letter was discussed with students using their vocabulary skills to promote the purchase of something they really would like to have. If it is going to be an economic-awareness activity, students could research a possible holiday gift and calculate the cost for purchase, shipping costs, and taxes, or they might also calculate and compare what it would cost to get to the mall from their home or school to purchase the gift. They could also conduct research by comparing their first choice item with another and calculate the differences in quality, size, or other criteria you set together. Comparison charts can be fun and useful to make and share with classmates. Perhaps you have a "big-ticket" item you would like to purchase for the library as a copy machine or 3-D printer. Ask students to help creating a bulletin board with a graph showing the choices, costs, advantages, disadvantages, and reasons for purchasing. Schoolwide voting or input from students can guide you toward the purchase you would like to make.

Students can become aware of the cost of living by comparative shopping in newspaper ads. The costs of automobiles and houses are usually the features of Sunday papers. Students can bring these from home, and being placed in groups of three or five, they can figure out which car dealer has the best bargain for a vehicle they would choose to buy. One grandmother asked her two 14-year-old grandsons to help her choose the features she would need on her new car for her type of driving, local on city streets with no plans for long-distance driving on freeways, and she was going to take them with her when she went to buy that car. Their "research" was done exclusively on their cell phones.

Another expense for students after high school is planning to buy a home. Homes can be researched by size and amenities. Is a home with a two-car garage more expensive than a home with a one-car garage? Or comparisons can be made from ads for apartments and the differences in amenities offered in those brief ads.

Those students whose parents can afford a summer vacation could be involved in planning that vacation. Alternative fun activities are also suggested for those who might not be going out of town for an extended vacation away from home.

The cost of living has a great deal of impact on where a student might choose to seek a job, and tying career choice to economics of location for that job is both a part of career and financial literacy. Students in these grades are mature enough to take these both into consideration, and they are well able to begin accepting their responsibility for living in a democracy.

Civic Responsibility

The library is an excellent place to invite students to recognize and take charge of their civic responsibilities and learn what they must do to be good citizens. A basic learning is "Do unto others as you would have others do unto you," which begins with treating each other fairly. It is never too early to continue any discussion about bullying that might be happening to any student. You may well be that trusted person who could listen to a student in the library where that conversation would be easier perhaps than during the school day in the classroom.

Students can begin to realize what their government provides for them and their families. One of the best ways to teach governance and responsibility is to put some choices on students; if these are *their* rules, then they might be more likely to follow them. Discussing which rules might work best and the reasons why they might be necessary is the best way to confirm the need for the rule.

Gather your principal and teachers together early in the school year and let them know that this year you would like the students to review rules for the library. Solicit their ideas and get their support so that the whole school is behind you in this process. Depending upon the time you have to do this, you could limit your exercise to one grade level as the "House of Representatives" that will make the rules with "constituent" input from other classes. Then let all the students vote on them. The class that designs the rules can learn how to gather data, analyze them, and prioritize and create a list of useful rules for library behavior and accountability. The other students in the school provide the input and participate in a school vote, which becomes a civics lesson in itself.

The members of the House of Representatives will research existing rules, the reason for them, and the degree of success each seems to be having. If something does not seem to be working, constituents can be asked to make suggestions just as citizens call their representatives to make suggestions, and wording of the rules can be discussed.

Students will consider the adage that "If you make a rule, you need to decide what to do when the rule is broken and what the penalty will be." Practicing give and take, discussing what is considered acceptable behavior, and affirming the value of the library space allow students to grapple with the concepts of fairness, openness, diversity, and accountability. They may begin to understand that keeping track of the consequences for breaking the rules and making sure any penalties are carried out are more difficult than just expecting students to be responsible without established rules.

It will be up to the House of Representatives, the original rule makers, to provide examples of situations students might encounter in the library so that voters will understand the reasons and vote responsibly. Do they think it is necessary to charge fines or to restrict the number of books or other items a student may take home at one time? If the voters decide not to charge fines or restrict the number taken, it becomes their responsibility to consider how to encourage students to return them when they are due. If they decide the checkout time period is longer than one or two weeks and books out for more than two weeks are subject to recall when requested by someone else, then they need to decide how long is reasonable for the person who has the book to return it. To place this into absolute reality, perhaps you or the principal will have the role of "president" for library laws and will have the veto power for any rule.

Letting students establish the anticipated behavior while they are in the library gives them an opportunity to talk about what is distracting, and everyone should have a chance to add to this discussion. You can begin with a small group process in individual classrooms or during regular library time with each class to decide what is good, what is disturbing to others, and what is necessary for all to accomplish what they need to do in the library. Even fourth-grade students are amazing with their perceptions of what it takes to be a good citizen in the library and what is necessary for them to be successful. It takes the onus from your shoulders and places behavior where it belongs and with those who can control it themselves.

Once these decisions on rules and behavior are made, the entire school can hold an election and vote for their choices. Having students campaign for one of these choices would add to their knowledge of how candidates get elected or laws get passed. This type of in-school interaction gives students a vocabulary from which to look into their communities for other examples of rule creation and consequences.

Civic responsibility includes learning in more depth about those persons who work in governance at the school level or in city positions. At the school level, students can under-stand that the school board is responsible for many decisions that affect them, including hiring teachers and other personnel in the school and enforcing any state requirements for student performance. At the city level, governance includes mayor and city council or county officials. Knowing what these people do helps students begin to understand a commitment to civic responsibility. Hearing any of these persons describe their positions is helpful even at this level. Similar to the list described in Chapter 1, keeping a list of these officials for your use and for the use of your teachers, should they need to hear from one of these persons, is most helpful.

Issues may come up within school districts that require community input, including school closures, program changes, or budget concerns. Interested parents may attend school board meetings in order to gain more information and to provide their own input. Most fourth-grade students are capable of understanding issues about their school and its program, and they could certainly attend a school board meeting with their parents. Should any students attend, you could ask for a report back to the class on the process and procedures held at such a meeting as part of your discussions on communities, community helpers, and/or government. Were they limited in the amount of time they could speak? What issues did they address? What seemed to be the opinion of the crowd, pro or con for the issue?

Taking advantage of the many things that go on in a school and community, you and classroom teachers can arrange some instruction time toward awareness of these current events and creating assignments where students are allowed to ask questions, develop opinions, and practice their information-literacy skills of searching out information, evaluating it, and reflecting upon it. For example, learning about the governing officials for the community—the mayor, city council, and the county commissioners—and how they are appointed or elected can be discussed if some event in the community brings them to attention. While it may naturally come up in election season, do not limit your-self to only that time to have great discussions on election procedures, including discus-sing how to decide to run for office; what candidates need to have, including funding; how to get the word out; and how to prepare for debate and issue discussions. Teachers may know those students who have a parent or other family member who is a government official; they could be asked to visit the school to talk about what their responsibilities for the community are. Other students may know who these persons are because they see them at events. All of these experiences help set the stage for the next level of school.

Helping students learn about those offices, agencies, and other resources their families might need to solve a challenge in their lives can be helpful. Any of these can be found with a quick cell phone or computer search if someone knows what to ask. Some numbers, such as fire department, ambulance, and police, are in your school office for emergencies. Your local public library will have numbers to call for many government agencies and community support groups that help families in times of need among many others. Helping students generate a list stored on their cell phones may provide families who are less able to find this information have it available to call. Potential numbers include, among others, who to call to get an ownerless animal collected, where to report a lost bicycle, and many more. 📝

Civic responsibility includes your students knowing what to do in case of emergency for themselves and for their family and friends. Today's reality includes knowing how to handle oneself during a violent intrusion, as well as many natural disasters. A great library parent evening can include speakers who can help students and their families prepare an emergency plan for just such disasters. Students need to know who to call in case of emergencies at home or if they are away from home and even in the school. Reinforce that calling 911 can be crucial and that students can do this when a true emergency arises. Parents should give students a phone number of a reliable neighbor and a close relative. The other number to call in case of an emergency for students with pets is the number of their veterinarian. The school nurse will be helpful in explaining care for nonthreatening health situations at home such as an elderly grandparent or recuperating parent. So many students have cell phones these days that placing emergency numbers into them so that they are immediately available is something librarians can encourage parents to do with their children. Contacting help in an emergency and then abiding by any instructions given by responders is also a civic duty.

This is an excellent time to introduce students to the superintendent and school board and any city officials, including the mayor, with whom you can get to visit. Have the students prepared with the issues they might address and how they might address them. It may be possible to invite a government official to visit your school. 📝 Make sure that you find officials to visit from across gender, race, and other diverse lines. Everyone should find role models who participate in the government. For an interesting activity, introduce students to a woman who in the end of the nineteenth century was active in the fight for women's rights. 📝

These types of activities help students see that government officials are here to work for them and they are accessible to their constituents. As local or state and national elections are held, and if a polling site is held at your school, take a moment to show students what a polling area looks like. All this begins the process of encouraging students to be responsible, informed citizens and vote.

While it may seem too soon to talk to students about registering to vote and voting, having a local politician, county commissioner, school board member, or city mayor or council member come to the school and talk with students will allow the entire school to participate. If field trips are heavily funded, visiting one of these offices would be a good introduction to the political process.

If you are collaborating with your social studies teachers at the beginning of a discussion of the Constitution, you are a part of the planning and will have a voice in what is being taught. Otherwise, you can offer some interesting programming to reinforce what your students are learning in these classes.

Helping students understand both government and how it works and how someone might begin to prepare to help a government official can be fun using interesting activities. A little about how the government works and how someone can plan to help a government official in his or her duties can be an interesting challenge.

By sixth grade, students in self-contained classrooms should be ready to hold an election for president of the classroom. If your principal and teachers agree with the premise, this election can be held for a shorter period of time, perhaps six weeks, allowing more than one student to assume that position for a shorter period of time; it will provide opportunities for other students to try their skills in leading meetings. It is a good time to let them think if they should want to be president one day.

Practicing leadership begins early and allows students to learn how to lead and also how to understand the pitfalls that can challenge the leader. For instance, what should a student leader do when they see a wrong that should be made right? If it is happening in their school, an immediate solution should be found. If it is as broad as what a national event may generate, discussion involves more than the classroom or even the school. For students to leave school to protest requires planning to make it work, always remembering that appropriate protesting can lead to change. The use of social media in gathering support for any cause and organizing protests happens all around the country and has involved high school and even younger students. Discussions about appropriate uses of social media and its influence bring back the earlier mention of bullying. It also allows discussion of the civic responsibility of accepting people, parents, and other students who are different and the many ways those differences can be seen and others that cannot be seen.

In closing civic responsibilities, students in grades 4–6 can learn a great deal about how organizations support students and can visualize the roles they will play in paying it forward. They will understand that it does take a village to raise a child.

Students completing the sixth grade are ready for the next level, junior high school. The next chapter covers what happens in grades 7 and 8.

Suggested Activities

Responsibilities for the Librarian

1. When you create a "learning center" area in your library, you can rotate activities throughout the year. Learning centers provide students the opportunity to test their knowledge in a less stressful climate. Many of the activities will seem more fun than learning. This kind of learning center held during library time can help you expand collaboration with teachers because this provides the opportunity for both of you to teach students how to sort carefully through information, finding bias and inaccuracies. Learning centers can encompass any topic and can fill many teaching objectives across content areas.

   Learning centers can introduce sources of information available in the library, practice in accessing the online catalog, and how to find those resources on the shelves as well as in the databases the library owns.

2. Checking for the usefulness of any resource is the beginning step in conducting research, a basic information-literacy assignment. Students need to find information that addresses their question. They then move to an assessment of what is useful, relevant, and accurate and finally move to fact-checking of sources. You can have students work in groups of four or five to create their own checklist for checking facts and generate a list of questions prioritizing their top two, three, or more. While this can be done by individuals, this is better accomplished with students in groups who will help each other decide what is needed to check accuracy. If students need help in creating their lists, you can start this process with suggesting some of the following questions: Who wrote the information? Where can you check facts in this information? (While *Wikipedia* is often shunned in the research process, it is an easy spot to begin to fact-check.) How up to date is the information? Who published this information? Does the information seem biased? If so, where could you find an alternative position or additional information? If the information is an electronic resource, who or what organization sponsors this site? At the end of the exercise, groups share their lists to arrive at a whole-class list. Once this list is ready, they can apply it to any research topic they are assigned. Post their questions on a bulletin board for all to use.

   Working in groups, students can share their ideas and help one another to pick their top three or four and begin to research with those sources. Be sure to reflect at the end of the day: Which sources worked well? Which ones did not? Ask them to write the answers to the following questions: What did you learn? How did you learn it? You can use those questions from the Right Question Institute with every reflection you ask students to do.

3. Fill a box with construction paper, 4×6 envelopes, and colored pens and pencils. If students need to write thank-you notes for any event, they will find the supplies to do that on their lunchtime or before or after school.

4. Persuasive letter writing is an exercise when the ads for holiday gifts begin to appear. Suggest that they write a letter to their parents detailing the gift they might like to receive and the reasons this gift will be important, helpful, and useful for them. They carefully describe the exact model they want, including color, size, attachments, or any other accessory they want, where it might be purchased, the price options for the gift, and any alternatives for one particular brand or model. The persuasive words they will use need to make it important, helpful, and useful for them. Or, consider having them write ads for items not for themselves but for their school, a local hospital, or other cause they are interested in supporting.

Education Environment

5. Introduce an etiquette book to grade 4 and explain that these are rules written to help someone behave in an expected fashion in the United States. Mention that different rules may be in place in other countries, such as that it is extremely rude and even taboo to show the bottom of your feet to someone in Thailand, whose cultural mores say that the head is the highest part of the body and sacred, while the feet are dirty. If you have a student who is interested in what other countries might consider taboo, this student could do further research. For all, you will explain the proper way to shake hands with another to introduce yourself.

6. In the next two grades, this lesson can be expanded into how to introduce teachers to parents, and by grade 6, they should be able to write an introduction to use when a visitor is coming to the classroom to speak to the group.

When organizing a scavenger hunt during orientation, include having students introduce themselves to you and anyone who is assisting. They should both tell their name and shake hands. This may turn out to be difficult for many students and a revelation for any student who had never before done an introduction. It was a fun, easy way to meet every student in each class and give them a chance to practice this important skill.

7. Providing students an opportunity to learn to work in groups is as simple as giving the topic to three or four students rather than individual assignments. If you ask students to research an occupation, assign a single occupation and let them pool what they already know and decide who will look up what information to confirm what they know and research what they need to find out. Then they can decide the type of person who would be interested in that type of job. If it is an assignment to compare occupations within a group, you could assign the group one profession—medical, service, or governmental—and let them find out the relationship between all the persons working in that institution or agency.

Career Information

8. Students can begin to research different occupations, gathering information about what these persons actually do, their salaries, the training they will need, the location where they will work, including city or state or even country, and what they wear to work, among other things; you and your students will decide what needs to be gathered. Explain that the information collected by students will be placed in a database for review throughout the fourth grade and then revised through additions to new vocations suggested when this is taught again in grades 5 and 6. You may wish to share your electronic database when these students enter junior high. Your database can also be a binder with each occupation listed, a drawing, and a few pertinent facts.

Students in grade 4 may be able to determine the types of professions on the basis of those they know. If they do not easily do this, here are some suggestions:

Agriculture: farm workers, dairy farmers, vineyard owners and workers

Arts: painters, sculptors, arts and crafts, owners of art galleries, museum docents

Commercial: groceries, department stores, travel agencies

Government: city, county, state, national

Helping: social work, medicine, physical trainers, librarians, teachers at all levels

Manufacture: various industries

Medical: doctors, dentists, nurses, specialists, veterinarians

Military: U.S. Air Force, U.S. Army, U.S. Coast Guard, U.S. Marines

Research: laboratory technicians, chemists in pharmaceutical companies, archeologists

Recreation and performance: sports teams, musicians, actors, vocalists

Support: office staff, computer technicians, building engineers, restaurant staff

Transportation: airlines, trains, buses, cab drivers

The Texas Workforce Commission offers a fun packet of worksheets called "Careers Are Everywhere" that they adapted from the *Elementary Career Awareness Guide* by North Carolina SOICC: https://lmci.state.tx.us/shared/CareersAreEverywhere.asp. You can use these to spark activities that you can use in the library: self-assessment, roles we play in life, and much more. One that is particularly interesting (p. 29) and can be accomplished in the library asks students to create an "assembly line" for making a greeting card. Each student adds his or her own bit to the card. After the card is finished, discussion continues about the pros and cons of making 20 or 50 or 100 cards this way.

9. Find recordings of the college "fight" songs and their alma mater songs for the colleges and universities in your state or for any college that a student's sibling or relative attends. If any students have a pennant from a college, ask them to bring it to the library to display. Discuss the school colors and how they are used in the sport's equipment, the band uniforms, and the cheerleader attire. When these institutions are nearby, this introduces students to the possibility of attending a college without moving too far from home.

   Sports teams in your state and any neighboring states may have televised events that students will watch. Students who attend such an event on campus with parents or other relatives or friends can share any information they are given while they are at the event.

10. Arranging for students even this young to hear about what they can learn at a higher education institution makes it a reality that they might attend instead of an impossible dream. It will generate discussion about what it means to get a college degree and why one is needed for some of the occupations your students are already researching.

Economic Awareness

11. You can suggest collaborating with your math teachers to use the lessons from the FDIC's *Money Smart* program for middle grades: https://catalog.fdic.gov/money-smart-young-people-grades-6-8-downloadable. However, there are many places that you can adapt workshops, lunchtime programs, or after-school events in the library. For example, Lesson 10 talks about identify theft.

    Collaborating with your teachers or in your library programming, you can adapt these into video announcements for the morning broadcast of the school news or bookmarks with tips or bulletin board tips.

12. If your city is large enough to have a weekly section with houses for sale, students can use this information for this project. You may also visit your local realtor for flyers for 10 houses they have on the market. Students can note differences in what houses cost based upon their location, size, and other statistics that are comparable on the information you provided for them. Sixth graders may be able to calculate the amount they might have to borrow to buy the house and then look at the interest they would pay over time.

    If most of your students live in multifamily dwellings, then looking at apartment rentals can help students understand how much paying rent will take from the salary of their potential employment. While this may seem premature for this age, it may help students understand the challenges their parents face.

13. Ann Schuster, a National Board Certified Teacher Librarian from Overland Park, Kansas, supports her fourth-grade teacher with a "travel guide" activity that

requires students to budget their money as they take a trip to the landmark of their choice:

My 4th grade teacher began this unit by giving the students a packet (yes, paper and pencil) primarily so they could do their calculations. She customized a lesson on U.S. Landmarks she found on Pinterest (http://Pinterest.com/scangelosi).

Here was the introduction:

"You are going to visit a landmark in the Midwest region. You will have to travel to the location of the landmark by car or plane, stay in a hotel and pay for the cost of meals and admission to the landmark, if required. Your budget is $x (teacher can set amount)."

This was preceded by a discussion of what landmarks are/what they represent and determination by students of the Midwest landmark they would like to visit.

> For a project like this, the National Park Service is an excellent resource for locating monuments and other landmarks. Check out NPS.gov.

The students needed to determine whether it was more budget-friendly/time expedient to travel by car or plane using a given price per gallon of gas, Google Maps to determine mileage, and two airline Websites and dates to travel; which hotel could accommodate them for two nights picking at least a three-star hotel and where they could eat.

Our teacher used Class Kick to post links to database sites on our library web page to investigate landmarks, Google Maps, and other needed information. I assisted with this as well as providing print resources. We then scheduled library times for the co-taught lessons.

Students were given the choice of presenting via iMovie or Flipgrid, Post Card (all our student iPads have the PhotoCard app) or travel brochure. A reflection document is available at the end of the project.

Students who will not be going on extended vacations can still look at how much it costs to go to a movie. If they have a certain amount of money to spend, can they pay for the movie and have popcorn and a soft drink? Or, if the class was going on a field trip to a museum, how much would it cost to buy lunches to take from the school cafeteria? Using the Question Formulation Technique (QFT) process can facilitate this activity by letting students ask the questions they need to know in order to get to that movie or museum.

> This QFT process is described in Chapter 2, Activity 7. Using the QFT process from rightquestion.org can be accomplished by learning the process from their website or their book: *Make Just One Change*. This simple step-by-step process teaches students to brainstorm the questions that occur to them and then gives them a process for identifying them, prioritizing them, and allowing them to decide which question they want to know most about.

While not a new idea, it still offers students an excellent financial-literacy exercise. Place students in groups of three or four and have them make a shopping list of items they might need for a party for 10 friends. Then have them view ads in the newspaper to see how much it would cost to buy the items they think they will need. It is always good to save the inserts from weekend newspapers, which may have more ads than a daily newspaper has. This can be used with buying clothing to visit a location that has a very different climate than the students are experiencing at the time of your exercise. It may be snowing in Boston, but the weather in Hawaii is a constant temperature. If students wanted to go skiing in Vermont in January, they would need an entirely different wardrobe.

Civic Responsibility

14. The list of offices and phone numbers in Chapter 2, p. 30, can be used to begin your list. For these grades, addresses are added, and they can be located on a map of the city. Bus routes to arrive at the offices can be found, and distances to walk from the school to those locations can be an identifying exercise as well as a math problem: How long would it take to walk from the school to that location if you walked a mile in 10 minutes?

15. Working with teachers, help students create an electronic, easily updated, and printed—if a hard copy is needed—list of their important phone numbers, beginning with 911 as the emergency number to call and when to call it and how to make sure they are understood, staying on the line to give further instructions. Then those numbers to call when it is not an emergency, beginning with their home number; parents may have suggestions for numbers their students should have available. Then help them decide if the best place is their cell phone or another location.

16. With your principal's assistance and encouragement of teachers in your school, plan a visit from a government official to your school. If this level seems too primary for national or state officials, a member of the local city council or the school board would be a great substitute. Information about this official is posted on bulletin boards throughout the school. This person may be able to garner media attention, which will help bring affirmative attention to your school, to the education of students, and to the teaching and learning going on in your school. Students will need to craft a persuasive letter to the official and help plan what they will want to share with the official. Then they will need to write thank-you notes for that person's attendance.

17. Read Kate Hannigan's *A Lady Has the Floor: Belva Lockwood Speaks Out for Women's Rights* (Honesdale, PA: Calkins Creek, 2018) and ask students the following questions:

    • What is the Supreme Court?

    • Why was it unusual for a woman to plead a case before the Supreme Court?

18. Sponsor a Constitution Day Poster Contest and enter your top posters into the national contest at https://www.constitutionfacts.com/constitution-poster-design-contest/.

This is sponsored by the Government Information for Children (GIC) Committee (American Library Association [ALA]) and Constitutionfacts.com. Display them around the library before September 17, Constitution Day, and before sending them in.

Another fun project to celebrate the Constitution is to make American Flag pinwheels: https://constitutioncenter.org/media/files/American_Flag_Pinwheels.pdf. Host a pinwheel parade around the school. Have students hold on to their pinwheels in their class or the library and host another parade on Election Day in November.

Have students create a banner to display in the parking lot the day before the election stating, "Tomorrow is election day! Vote!" Two students can hold up the banner while the others hold up their pinwheels.

19. Ben's Guide to the U.S. Government (https://bensguide.gpo.gov/) offers easy-to-understand explanations of how the government works. Consider creating a scavenger hunt of the site with prizes for all.

20. Read Judith St. George's *So You Want to Be President* (New York: Philomel Books, 2000, illustrated by David Small and awarded the Caldecott Medal) to the class. If you do this at all three grade levels, you will want to prepare more difficult questions.

   • Name as many presidents as you can.

   • Who is the president now?

   • What must you do to become the president?

   • How might you help someone who was running for president?

   Do not forget that the "Presidents Song" is a fun way to teach the order of the presidents. Check out YouTube versions: https://www.youtube.com/results?search_query=presidents+song+for+kids.

21. Have both a LGBTQ flag and an American flag to show. Read *Pride: The Story of Harvey Milk and the Rainbow Flag* by Rob Sanders (New York: Random House, 2018, and illustrated by Steven Salerno). Be prepared to share the centerfold with all the different people holding the Pride flag so they can identify who these people represent. Ask students the following questions:

   • What was Harvey's dream? (Equality for all, and what does that mean?)

   • What did he first use to tell his dream? (Horn.)

   • What was his idea? (A march and a big flag.) What do you know about marches?

   • What is the difference between a march and a parade?

- How many stripes did his first flag have? How many now? What colors?

- How many stripes does our American flag have, and why that number?

- Who are the people in the centerfold?

- Show the picture of the White House. Why is it not white?

22. With the approval of the principal and the help of the teachers, interested parents and students in your school could identify the many opportunities available in their town or in their area of the larger city to participate in after-school activities that are available. Once the list is completed, they could plan an afternoon fair for students and their caregivers to come to school to find out about these opportunities that are low or no cost. They would invite representatives to host a table, sharing their opportunities for recreation such as Boys and Girls Clubs, Boy Scouts, Girl Scouts, Campfire Girls, the public library, sports teams, YMHA, YMCA, and YWCA. Invite students who participate in these activities to act as hosts for the representatives, sharing their enjoyment of the activity.

Suggested Resource for Further Information

Volkman, John D. *Collaborative Research Projects: Inquiry That Stimulates the Senses.* Westport, CT: Libraries Unlimited, 2008.

Note

1. American Association of School Librarians. *National School Library Standards: For Learners, School Librarians, and School Libraries* (Chicago, IL: ALA Editions, 2018), 67.

Chapter 4

Surviving While Teaching:
The Challenge of Junior High,
Grades 7–8

What a chaotic and exciting time junior high is for students, teachers, and parents. This chapter refers to junior high as seventh and eighth grades. The configuration of this level of education varies from state to state and even city to city with some "middle schools" covering grades 6–8, others 7–8, with others ranging from 6 to 9. Whatever the format, these are the students eager to become teens.

Junior high students may be characterized by wild bursts of energy, competing with extreme exhaustion and the larger amounts of food they need. Many parents remark on the effortless ability of their growing teens to "eat them out of house and home." The disparity in maturity growth at this age causes many teens to flounder as they begin to unravel their feelings of sexuality and identification. Eager to be on their way to adulthood, many young teens turn to their peers for guidance and acceptance, whereas before they would go to parents or teachers.

It is a testing period for students to see what it is like to be independent, and some of those tests will look almost comical to an adult when the students are so serious. This is easy to spot as they start mimicking what their favorite music group is wearing. The experiments with makeup and clothing can be startling. Then those trips arranged by the school to give students an opportunity to spend a few days visiting their state capitol or a historic site bring out the best and the worst behaviors. Some get homesick and try to hide that, assuming a blasé attitude about what the guide is saying. Eating in a restaurant, in a more formal atmosphere than they face at home, may make them watch others just to understand how to act. Many will try to stay awake and bother anyone who is trying to sleep. Others may cling to best friends as if they were life preservers. Keeping track of students and helping students keep track of their belongings are intensified by their need to be responsible when they have not really mastered how that is supposed to happen.

Entering junior high is a memorable step, and these young students are at an age when many teachers, parents, and other adults find them to be at their most difficult to try to reach or teach. Some psychologists say that their brains have been working very hard in their earlier years, and now these brains need rest and are sleeping, waiting for the next push. Similar to when they were cranky babies just before a "cognitive leap,"[1] teenage moodiness can be disconcerting. They can move from acting with 5-year-old behavior to 40-year-old in a glance. Texting is constant, and both subjects and recipients of those texts feel an entire range of emotions that can be crippling. At the other end of this spectrum is the eighth-grade leader, a boy who is literally chased by all the girls in junior high, who when he attends the school dance makes sure he asks as many different females as possible, including his teachers and the girl with cerebral palsy who must trade her supports for his hands, to dance. These early teenagers are equally a delight and energy-driven students for whom you and your library can offer much.

Responsibilities for the School Librarian

As with previous chapters and those that follow, the suggestions and activities may seem to be impossible to carry out with the assignments already on your planning book. However, as you read through this chapter, consider which of those tasks can be given to a volunteer or a student if your junior high has a club period and you may have students who really want to work with you, especially when you make those tasks fun as well as helpful.

Then analyze the tasks to see which of those do directly impact teaching and learning in your school. When you are collaborating with teachers to provide research skills, they have a chance to make a difference. In the collaboration process, if you could make some suggestions to teachers to use some of the ideas in this chapter for them to make assignments, you will be exercising your leadership role. If you are teaching research skills outside what is needed in the classroom, then perhaps trading some of these will be acceptable. Many of these suggestions can be offered over the noon hour or at any other open time during the day. You can begin this by finding out what students are missing from their school lives.

The library is a well-placed center for students to come to meet within an engaging and encouraging environment that also happens to have the kind of information emerging teens need. If it is a relaxed environment, it will be easy to find out what students need. You can be present with materials students need and where they can, quietly, on their own if necessary, locate answers to important and personal questions. Keeping the library open and visible, with key phone numbers, website addresses, and local support groups at the ready will help keep the lines of communication open so that you can more ably support these students as they move into their teen years.

You are a very valuable part of schoolwide teams who can work to make assignments both challenging to their intellect and interesting to them so they want to complete these to the best of their ability. Collaborating with teachers to provide assistance with inquiry-based learning experiences and creating hands-on activities that offer students potential success and a continuing interest in the base-level knowledge they are being taught can also increase a desire to move into deeper research when their interest is piqued.

An underlying reason for encouraging inquiry-based assignments and hands-on activities is that for many students who are questioning why they need to remain in school, offering them alternative, meaningful experiences within and beyond the classroom can encourage them to remain in school until they graduate. It is a formidable assignment for adults, parents, teachers, and librarians to help students identify those skills and attitudes they will need to use to plan and accomplish goals they might not have thought possible.

Scholarships, internships, and work-study programs can be introduced in junior high as possibilities for any student, but for the student who may not make it to graduation, it is time to provide the foundation for a successful career after high school. Helping students create questions and find answers can be taught with the Right Question Institute's Question Formulation Technique (QFT) that has been mentioned in Chapters 2 and 3. Applying this to career information will be discussed later in the chapter.

While few will think of the librarian as a promoter of recreation or physical education, you can encourage the idea of physical activity as a lifelong goal for all. Working with the physical education teachers, and perhaps outside speakers for the library, these adults can share their stories. While physical education in junior high begins with organized exercise and participation in competitive games, as adults, these are continued by working out in a gym or enjoying bowling, swimming, and hiking or enjoying across a wide spectrum of physical activities.

Those students who have been taking private lessons on a musical instrument or voice will have the opportunity to join the band or chorus. If homemaking is a curricular area, it may also be open to boys as well as girls, and they will have an opportunity to learn something about cooking and diet. The cooking shows on television are great introductions to that possibility. Writing stories for English class can be transformed into 10-minute drama scenes with one or two chosen to share with parents at open house. These are but a few of the possible opportunities that can open doors for young people as they look at their futures.

You can become the go-to person when students need help or advice beyond finding the information for their report or other assignment. No formal appointment is needed as it might be to see the guidance counselor; with print, media, and online resources right at hand, the school librarian can be the one person who can be relied on to help. Your daily presence and a welcoming environment in the library allow students to talk to you quietly and confidently about in-school and out-of-school problems, knowing that you will not betray their trust. When necessary, you can ask if you can have any other person to help solve their problems. A quiet word to the counselor can be most helpful to students in trouble or with concerns.

Working with the school counselor, you can begin explaining what will be expected of high school students. Sponsoring a series of "open house sessions" for parents in the library or even offering individual discussions with students if they want to invite their parents to come to school is one activity the library could sponsor. Holding such information sessions at a time when parents are coming to school for open house night is another time, if planned with the teachers, and time is allocated for parents to come to the library for this type of information. Finding out which parents do not come to open house may point to those students who are most in need of guidance for their high school choices. Reaching all parents will be a joint effort between you, administrators, the classroom teachers, and students.

Junior high students and their parents need to be reminded of the opportunities for research and study at the public library. While students are in school all day every day with their library available, they may have an information need for their homework assignment, and the open spot after dinner is the public library. As you are planning your agenda for any meeting with parents, you may wish to invite the public librarian to join you.

> Melinda Bender of Thirteen and Green Library [Reading PA] invites the public librarians in to spread the word about reading and libraries. "I have had crafts for students and their families to make, plus check out books. I am thinking about having therapy dogs to come so students could read to them."[2] Holding scavenger hunts, mini-lessons on database use, or search strategies for parents, or offering dessert and juice are all ways to encourage visitors during a busy Open House.

> Karen Sue Sorenson of Petal High school has had success with giving parents coupons for their students, such as "fine forgiveness" or printing 10 pages for free in the library. "I have also created survival kits with information for parents on how to help their students including information on the library, databases available and how to access from home."[3]

Many parents, previously more active in school, begin to withdraw from helping at school, mistakenly thinking that their children do not want them there. When attendance at events such as open house and student performances begin to slip, getting parents to the school becomes the hardest part. You can create activities to entice them to come after a long day of work by providing events that use the products students created in library instruction sessions or during lunchtime or other school programming. Especially helping "at-risk" students gain some sense of success is essential because many of these junior high students are beginning to mark the time when they will be old enough to leave school. For some students, the kinds of activities found in the library are the only activities in which they are successful. Being able to share those projects and products can become a source of pride for students who might not get such attention elsewhere.

Collaborating with seventh-grade teachers early in the year will help you understand the learning styles and learning difficulties of their students, knowledge that you will keep as these students continue for the next semester and when they enter eighth grade. You will be able to help both teachers and students when you recommend resources for students so that they are successful with their assignments.

Not all students will participate in sports teams, music opportunities, or dramatics clubs. Finding students who would like to help in the library will give you some needed help and also give them the opportunity to take a leadership role with their peers. Given extra orientation to the library's databases will allow them to help students with their searches and give them that special place where they can shine.

You are that teacher who is aware of the curriculum being taught in each class to all the students while they are in junior high. This makes you the go-to leader in the Education Environment.

Education Environment

From the beginning of seventh grade, the goal is to prepare students for the next step: high school. In some schools, an open house orientation is given to incoming students to take a look into the classrooms that they will be in starting in the fall. Making sure the library is on the tour and opening the doors wide to offer something of interest will let these prospective students see that, from their very first day on campus, there is a place that they know they are welcome. Many new seventh-grade friendships begin in the library and continue throughout their secondary school years.

These two years lead into the four-year high school experience, and it is time to introduce parents and students to that experience. Work with counselors at your school and the high school where students will attend to explain the opportunities for continuing their education. Reality is that these students will face some great changes in the school day from what they experienced in their first six grades. One of the major changes includes those break times in the school day.

In elementary school, recess was the way that students engaged in physical activity: letting off energy through unstructured but safe play. Starting in junior high, physical activity is accomplished through a more advanced, more organized exercise class. Activities may become more strenuous and can make those students who are less athletic dread this class. Games that involve learning new skills—requiring coordination and prior experience or needing to learn new concepts, such as the rules of many sports, or not knowing how to swim—can be difficult for children who have missed opportunities that were not available to them through their home life. Yet, junior high can provide those opportunities, and seventh grade is an excellent starting point for those who need to meet this challenge that could lead to physical activities continued throughout their adult lives.

Many students will move into a competitive sports program. When districts are large enough or the population area is dense enough, football, basketball, baseball, soccer, and volleyball games are played between teams, and swimming meets and tennis matches are scheduled. Those students who have the ability to participate in sports may be able to participate in team sports from junior high through high school and be able to transfer that skill into a college scholarship. It is an uncertain path, but one that needs to be shared as a possibility for those who are talented and interested in pursuing this route.

The band, orchestra, and choir members may participate in city- or district-wide concerts, and they may begin to compete as individuals in music contests. Meeting fellow musicians from other schools broadens minds, and debating those with perspectives far different from home informs young students that the world is big and there are many things to consider. These activities set the stage for writing those college applications, as well as scholarship requests.

While more and more schools are getting rid of lockers, learning how to handle school materials is a part of the junior high experience. Learning that "magical" process for opening lockers, keeping them organized, and remembering to keep books and other important items there between classes, as well as remembering to bring those needed to class, can be important steps in gaining responsibility. Students who move in and out of classrooms must get to and from lockers and to the next class between the bells. It allows them very little time to talk with the teacher either before or after class. This makes the library the place in the building that remains the same throughout their junior high experience, their home away from home.

Seventh grade is a time for students to adjust to the schedule that will follow them for the rest of their K–12 education. What began in grades 4, 5, and 6, the separating out of many of the content areas into single classes, is begun in earnest in junior high, and their "home" classroom may only be a brief gathering beginning the day to confirm attendance. The new schedules of the seventh-grade students begin to help them identify those courses and content areas that they like, do well or not so well, and by providing them with new experiences, can open many new doors to content areas that they knew little about before this year. This sets the stage for the next grade when students begin preparing for high school. This does not happen in a steady progression for all students.

Junior high is that bridge facing many low-achieving students who are obviously lagging behind classmates. For them, school has little relationship to their lives, and they and their teachers find few solutions, making this the "waiting" period until they drop out of school. It may seem frustrating to teachers and counselors who are trying to build a mechanism to encourage these students to remain in school, but at this point, it is essential.

Students who have accepted that they are "unable to learn," or see little reason to study or try to succeed as students, can be hard to reach, and junior high can be a last-chance opportunity to help these students see new opportunities. Finding any class or activity to interest them will not be easy but is critical in these two grades so that when they enter high school, they have a positive plan for success. Working to overcome long-standing family norms that suggest success is unattainable works only with relentless support and small steps just to encourage these students to find those things that interest them. If this fails, they will become the same as adults as their parents.

Trying to build a climate of hope for students who have learning challenges and those who have always lived in poverty, in a negative or harmful home environment, or in homes where education is not a priority, is not likely to be something that teachers who have grown up in middle-class homes can begin to envision. It takes the concentrated efforts of the entire school to create solutions and to offer hope for these students while encouraging them to build the skills they need to become successful in adult or "real" life. For example, for those students who are very good with technology, have them help you establish a geek squad that will allow them to assist you in helping both teachers and students. They might like to volunteer to help behind the circulation desk at lunch hour or before and after school. Others might enjoy helping create a display.

"Real life" can mean that some students attend underperforming schools, are at risk because of socioeconomic factors, or face family challenges every day, making it hard to even get to school some days. "Two race/ethnicities are in the lowest quartiles of family socioeconomic status (SES) which is an index score of the family's relative social position based on the parents' education, occupational, prestige, and family income."[4] A report of the National Center for Education Statistics[5] in February 2015 shows that the percentage of ninth graders who dropped out of school between fall 2009 and spring 2012 is 4.3 percent Black, 3.5 percent Hispanic, and 2.1 percent white, while only .3 percent were Asian students. Another 2.7 percent of "other" included American Indian/Alaska Native, Native Hawaiian/Pacific Islander, or "more than one race." The percentage of students in the lowest SES quintile was 4.7: 4.1 percent were in the second quintile; 2.5 percent were in the third quintile; and 1.6 percent were in the fourth quintile. Only .6 percent of students were in the highest SES. This disparity brings up a whole array of social issues that teachers, administrators, counselors, and librarians face each day as they work to build successful programs to meet the needs of their students.

When any students arrive at this level with reading, writing, and comprehension problems, they can easily fall even farther behind their classmates. This is especially true for those who attend lower-performing schools. When test scores are the measure, teachers are reluctant to deviate from the prescribed curriculum. Working with teachers to identify students and matching their needs with volunteers and tutors will help increase the students' skills and also send a message that every student is important. Sometimes it is another student at the junior high or a nearby high school student who is signed up for community service. Contact your local public library teen librarian to see how you can collaborate with programs that are already in place there, or if there are none, see if there might be ways to join together to create ways to meet these students with tutors at school or at the library.

Thinking about future courses to be taken in high school begins in junior high. "What is offered in the high school curriculum that will prepare me to work when I graduate? Do they have a vocational track? If I am planning to go to college, should I take a language class instead of a music class? Should I take any requirement such as the visual and performing arts requirement now, or later? What about sticking with math?" Students in junior high may be introduced to classes they never thought of taking; some schools have investigative "wheels" or required semester-long classes that expand their educational world. Whatever the style of scheduling a school has, being able to choose at least one course of interest can make a difference in how students feel about school and their future.

The educational environment has explained your role as a leader in helping all students have success in junior high. An additional challenge is to help counselors and teachers share career information with students throughout the school year.

Career Information

Few students at this age are giving serious thoughts to their careers; yet, it is time to do that because career choices affect required learning to meet those requirements, and this affects their choices for courses in high school. General information about occupations is available to share with all students to help them understand these challenges in their lives. The competencies they have directly affect what careers they may choose. This begins the time for students to assess their competencies.

After assessing their competencies, students may begin to record them by creating an educational planner that will provide them with a record that they can update over the next six years of schools. An example of a planner, "Career Components," a template created by Rosanne Cipollone of Pittsburgh, Pennsylvania, is shown below. She also suggests students take the career self-assessment inventory on pacareerzone.org. This provides career choices according to their interest. They can choose one or two careers and research them on bls.gov.

Reproducible 4-1

Name: _____

Career Components

Tasks (O*Net) or Nature of the Work (Occupational Outlook Handbook): (what you do on a daily basis)

1.	5.
2.	6.
3.	7.
4.	8.

Work Environment: Describe your workplace conditions: good and bad points

1.	3.
2.	4.

School Subjects: (subject in college or trade school)

1.	3.
2.	4.

Special Skills and/or Abilities: (O*Net)

1.	5.
2.	6.
3.	7.
4.	8.

Education Levels: How much education does your career require?

_____

_____

License or Certificate? Does this career require a special license or certificate?

_____

_____

Job Outlook or Need in the Future for this Career: Is there a big need for people in your occupation? Why or why not?

_____

_____

_____

Earnings: What is your salary?

_____

_____

Related Occupations:

_____

_____

_____

Students can also begin to gather information about various careers available and can maintain this list electronically in the library so that it can be updated as often as needed.

Even as society demands a high school diploma and beyond, there are other opportunities for students for whom the "regular" K–12 environment does not work. Home schooling, continuation, or other alternative schools exist in some districts or offer an alternative path to graduation. For those who insist that their own path is to leave school, they need to be made aware that the General Equivalency Diploma (GED) can be taken when they are 18 years old or other state-supported exams that allow students to leave after tenth grade. Finding locations in your area will be helpful to them, and they may be able to give this information to any family member who did not finish high school.

California has an alternate test, California High School Proficiency Exam (CHSPE), that a 16-year-old can take to graduate early. The decision to leave school or take an alternative path for completing an education should be taken in consultation with parents, teachers, and counselors. Few of these choices are available to junior high students, and they should be encouraged to stay in school until graduation. Much discussion can center at this point on future goals, career paths, and the many ways one can enter those careers. Career information becomes more focused as students learn the time commitment to prepare for careers, including those competencies that are taught in high school and then those requiring additional education and the number of years that path would take. For others, the competencies they will need may be available to them in their high school's vocational or certificate programs. They can begin now to identify those things that excite and motivate them so they can connect them with careers and the requirements for those careers.

If your high school does not have any training for trades or this is not offered with the school district, you can provide an introduction to places they may able to gain these skills and encourage them to talk with you as their librarian and ask the guidance counselor to help them schedule classes to allow them to do this before they graduate.

One way to give students a real picture of occupations is to arrange for them to meet people engaged in those professions. Working with the principal and counselors, you can arrange brown-bag lunches in the library and invite speakers to share information about their job.

If students are interested in a career in military service, the high school may have an Reserve Officers' Training Corps (ROTC) program. If not, there may be other out-of-school possibilities that can be pursued. If the high school does not have any training for trades or this is not offered within the school district, you can provide an introduction to places they may be able to gain those skills. They can then design their high school classes and perhaps start any of the training during part of the school day in their junior and senior years.

For students who are considering attending college after high school, they should be introduced to those Advanced Placement classes in high school. They can decide if they qualify, or if they wish to take these classes and the exams that accompany them, which will exempt them from those classes when they get to college. Some local universities or community colleges admit high school students, which can be a viable option for some students. Be sure to connect these students with their counselors to find out the admissions process for any of these programs. They will not be able to take these courses until they are in high school, but knowing that there are possibilities can help junior high school students understand their options.

Formal career education at the junior high can include counselor visits to classes and projects in class that ask for individual reflection on their future. Biography projects are ways that students can "try on" career ideas. The library will need narrative biographies so students have access to life stories of many successful people; many of these have overcome great obstacles to gain their success.

Junior high schools may have a number of clubs available for students to join that may help them develop skills, help others, and work together. Encourage students to join clubs that they might not think of, including debate, improv comedy, drama, or anime as well as the band, choir, cheerleading, and sports.

It may seem an insurmountable challenge, but helping one student at a time to succeed is the goal. You are well placed to provide that one-on-one smile that could begin a connection that lasts the two years of junior high. It is in the library where sharing information resources and activities could spark an interest in something that a student never knew existed.

Moving into junior high many years ago, a student discovered the makeshift television studio that the library created to produce a morning news broadcast. This student had no interest in school and was repeatedly sent out from various classes for inappropriate behavior. He was wickedly smart and probably too clever for junior high. But once he discovered that television camera, he was hooked. What started as one of the only ways he could connect with school, he created videos for most projects, borrowed the camera to take home and make his own movies, and proceeded to take all video-production classes throughout the rest of his secondary schooling. Many years later, the school librarian and "that kid" are still friends, and his successful career as a writer was honed by his very strange forays into television. Librarians can create the opportunities that students never thought possible.

For students to think about careers, they must think about the income those careers provide for them. Will it be enough to provide food, housing, clothing, transportation, and recreation, those things that are both necessary and essential for living a comfortable life. The next section discusses economic factors and helps you introduce your students to information and financial literacy.

Economic Awareness

Economic awareness aligns well with career information because it is necessary to answer questions such as "How much must I earn to sustain an individual or a family?" "If I want to get additional training or education after high school, what will that cost?" "How much does it cost to feed a family of four for a month?"

"Real-life" activities in these grades include the cost of things, identifying how to decide between one kind of purchase versus another, and based upon salary and expenses, which of these one can afford. The C3 Framework (p. 11) identifies the importance of understanding the economic decision-making process from individual purchases to global economics. Students will be studying economic ideas in their different classes. In history class they learn about innovation during the Renaissance, the founding of the United States, and the larger concepts of philosophy and the Enlightenment. These topics can be continued in the library, where students participate in activities about supply and demand, economic decision priorities that impact the way people live and gain an understanding of the global economics of trade. The Silk Road can be traced on a library map, with continuous additions from students throughout the week(s). On top of that route, the Slave trade can be marked, as can Marco Polo's routes. All these routes filled an economic purpose. How do we fill these same desires to trade today? These are interesting topics that can be practiced in the library through programming as well as coteaching with the classroom teachers. These are perfect for long-term units of study using lessons from government sites or economic organizations.

Some junior high students are beginning to want or need to earn their own money. Ideas for this age include cutting neighbors' grass or helping with gardening, babysitting, tutoring, or other informal means of employment. Most states allow students to work with work permits starting around age 15. To verify the requirement for your state, see https://www.dol.gov/whd/state/state.htm, with limits. Offering workshops on a variety of topics, including how to start up a small business, might be of use to these young entrepreneurs.

The reality of credit card debt is something that needs to be taught because most of these students have little, if any, idea of the reality of day-to-day costs of living. Some parents are well able to provide an excellent life for their children, while others at the other end of the spectrum cannot provide adequate food or housing. Discussing financial obligations through the use of credit cards is a neutral way to do this.

Becoming a good citizen in elementary school was mostly focused on learning about the various government offices that control the lives of citizens in the United States. Students at all levels must be made aware of their obligations as citizens within a democracy. Junior high students are ready to more than understand; they are ready to begin to practice.

Civic Engagement

Junior high schools often offer similar student-body activities as the high school. Spirit days, school dances, and other bonding activities allow students from many diverse elementary schools to meet and get to know their fellow students early in the school year. Those students who were leaders in elementary school will meet leaders from the other schools much as they will when they enter high school, and the dynamics can change. This will be quickly apparent when students begin to be part of elections within the school with student council or club chair elections. The library is an excellent place for students to come to create the posters and any flyers they might need to campaign for themselves or their candidate. It could even be the place for students to come to vote.

If your school does not have any opportunities for students to take leadership roles, why not? The argument that an election can create an elite group within the school can be lessened by having a variety of positions to elect, the length of time to hold the position, and the tasks for which the student is responsible. For instance, homerooms can choose the responsibilities for the "office," how to conduct the "election," and how long the "official" is to serve. "Rolling" officers can create opportunities for many students to participate in leadership.

Having elections in the school allows you to bring up the need for students to learn how to run meetings. The University of Utah FFA Chapter has an excellent quick guide to running meetings that can be used in any situation: https://chatham.ces.ncsu.edu/wp-content/uploads/2013/01/4-H_Leadership_2008-01pr.pdf?fwd=no. It would also be a good time to bring up the published guides such as *Robert's Rules of Order* and the role of a parliamentarian at a meeting. Assigning the task of this role will give a leadership opportunity and will also challenge the officers and the audience to be aware of the contents. Having students tune into a televised day in their state legislature or Congress can be used to see how the rules governing these groups are followed.

At this point, you may be thinking that this will mean you need to step into a leadership role to create an atmosphere where elections can be held. Even when this is already in place, trying to expand the leadership possibilities will require planning for a successful execution. You can start within the library. If you have students who work in a library club, you can have them rotate officers, perhaps every eight weeks. They can lead the club to help identify problems with any process within the library to help make any changes that will improve library service.

You might also hold an election for chair of your geek squad every eight weeks. These newly elected officers might be able to attract new students to the squad and decide who teaches the new members, who is assigned to work with teachers, and who is assigned to work with students in every homeroom or subject area. All this adds a little to the workload, but it provides excellent opportunities for students to test their capabilities and to shift from one skill to another.

If providing leadership opportunities goes beyond the library, teachers may be reluctant to help. After all, this is that most difficult age to harness the enthusiasm of some or generate any enthusiasm in other students. Organizing elections for other clubs is something that would require the support of the principal and other teachers. However, it is an excellent place to encourage students to do some of the decision making and to be able to practice what it is to lead a group. Not all students aspire to be leaders, but they need to have the opportunity to test the process, and this is a good place to start. Clubs in junior high need a sponsor who is willing to be active in helping students start, organize fairly, and create activities for each other that are safe, engaging, and useful and include everyone.

Students at this age will be aware of their parents' points of view on national and local issues (see Figure 4.1). Their opinions of who is acceptable and who is not are well ingrained. One way to help students create their own points of view and, at the same time, include parents in the process is to create an activity in the library that encourages family discussion.

Figure 4.1

As students begin to branch out, meeting new people who may be different from them in a variety of ways, they may begin to question their family values, which can be stressful or difficult, depending on how that questioning is perceived and/or handled. You might generate a wide variety of books and other resources that give varying points of view on issues, include stories from diverse perspectives, and include characters that face a variety of challenges. Biographies and memoirs begin to fill a place for these students who are just beginning that road to discovering their unique identity.

Parents' night in the library provides an opportunity to "lobby" for students to take an active role in meeting government officials both to share what is going on in the school and to make suggestions for improvement if there is a problem. Obviously, the depth of the problem will dictate, to a certain extent, whom to visit, what to say, and what response is to be expected. Students should be able to attend a school board meeting or county or city councils.

Attending a school board meeting or some event in city or county government will not involve as much planning as visiting a state or national official, but these are two groups of people who have widespread impact on citizens. If an issue is relevant to students and they could offer assistance in visiting a member of the state legislature or Congress, their presence and voice during the interview will be very important. Most officials enjoy being in the company of younger students and explaining what they do, how they feel about issues, and how important it is for young people to be interested and engaged in community, state, and national issues. Officials also enjoy having a picture in the local media, and that draws attention to your library too.

At the time of writing this book, citizens from all walks of life are gathering to march and hold important discussion on issues facing citizens today, including school shootings, blatant racism, bullying, and sexual harassment. These marches and meetings can become volatile and put up more walls than creating effective communication. As their older siblings march and organize, junior high students are watching and taking note. You can be a trusted adult to help organize information and offer speakers to come visit classrooms or libraries to help identify ways that these students can proactively help their communities with issues that are important to them. Facilitating deep discussions on hard issues is an important service that you, as a librarian, can take on with the help of the administration, teachers, counselor, and community members who work in community-building professions. Taking action by helping others can help these young people recognize that they too have an important role to play in their school and community.

Understanding the governance of our country is usually taught in the context of U.S. history. One of the most recognized officials is our president. Some teachers assign students to learn the names of all presidents. If students in your school are required to be able to name presidents, they may enjoy learning the "Presidents Song." When it is time to elect a president, it is time to learn about the electoral college and how the numbers may allow someone to have a greater popular vote but not win the presidency. This requires a knowledge of the different states and a little about their location. If your U.S. history students have to be able to identify where each state is located, you can show them how to practice with Ben's Guide[6] game "Place the State," which offers easy-to-understand explanations of how the government works. Consider creating a scavenger hunt of the site with prizes for all. Participants have to place state outlines in their proper place. You can then explain the difference between blue states and red states and discuss how the geography might have some influence on that factor.

Civic responsibility includes abiding by the laws governing them as students in their school and as citizens in this democracy. Legal issues regarding behavior can become more personal and relevant as they are now older. The law and the punishment for not abiding by the law are becoming more relevant now. It is a time to help students understand the outcome and any consequences of pranks they may think are harmless but which can change their lives in a very short time. The discussion of the long-range impact of posting messages on social media, graffiti, shoplifting, and destruction of property are all issues that need to be discussed as part of larger discussions on the roles and responsibilities of citizenship.

Studying government can include some activities that are fun. The national holidays often have parades and marching bands. In fact the music classes may feature these, and the junior high band students may be learning these in preparation for an appearance in a parade. Knowing the background of composers—John Philip Sousa may be the most prolific—can be shared in the library before such a holiday.

Not all holidays close banks and the post office, but they are equally important, and working with the art teacher, students can create posters to celebrate these days. Displaying them in the library, the school halls, and cafeteria can help students put those events into their consciousness.

The last challenge for students that grows as they mature is just how active to be. Should they march in a parade to support or reject an issue? As stated earlier, some students will join their parents in protests or meetings, while others will take on issues of importance to them and which may go against their family's values. Students in junior high are just beginning to see that there is a larger world than what they may have known in the past. It can be a difficult transition for some. Patience, information, and instruction on how to evaluate information will go a long way to helping young teens understand how they want to interact with others going forward. They will have this time to practice.

This chapter has given a view of the two very difficult years before transitioning into high school. The next chapter covers the first two years of high school.

Activities

Responsibilities for the Librarian

1. Plan an open house in the library to coincide with parents' night at the school and help provide parents with brochures from different government agencies that will highlight topics that impact junior high students today.

Educational Environment

2. The guidance counselor at the junior high can invite the counselors from the high school to come to eighth-grade classes to explain what the high school has to offer: Career and Technical Education (CTE) courses and higher education. Encourage students to diversify their schedules to take courses of interest as well as try out something new and interesting.

   Counselor visits could be supplemented with high school students from those various different course opportunities who organize small group discussions for students. They can be scheduled in school and after school and, whenever possible, with parents. This may need to be repeated at the beginning of ninth grade when students who were entering high school from another location will need this information before choosing their path.

   If the junior high is walking distance from the high school, classes could walk there for a planned visit.

3. Establish a geek squad that can accommodate some of your potential misfits. Showing these students that they have your trust in carrying out their assignments not only helps their teachers and peers with technology issues but also gives them a true sense of their worth. Make sure they are aware of privacy issues.

Career Information

4. Using the USA.gov YouTube channel, check out these occupation videos: https://www.youtube.com/playlist?list=PLDB4BCE9817AE7B43. These can be shown in the library at lunch just before you, as described in Activity 6, have a speaker come to the library to describe the kind of work that they do.

   You could use Rosanne Cipollone's suggestions as a handout for students who are investigating careers and need additional electronic locations.

Reproducible 4-2

Occupational Outlook Handbook

After choosing your career, find it on this website and print in "printer-friendly" format. Use this information along with the O*Net information to write your Career Research Paper.

> http://stats.bls.gov/search/ooh.asp?ct=OOH

O*Net: Occupational Informational Network

Type your career choice in the upper-right corner, select from career results, and then print. Use this information along with the Occupational Outlook Handbook information to write your Career Research Paper.

> http://online.onetcenter.org/skills/

Life Works—Health and Medical Science Careers

Everything you need to know if you are entering a career in the medical field. Complete with job description, education requirements, and interviews by actual people in the field.

> http://www.science.education.nih.gov/LifeWorks.nsf/feature/index.htm

Career One Stop

Contains videos about careers, career info, tools, and technology required for positions and special skills needed.

> http://www.acinet.org/

5. Adapting a lesson from Many Ways to Win: Teacher-Directed Activities (https://www.msjc.edu/cte/Documents/MWTW-Teacher-Directed-Activities%20MSJC.pdf), ask students to list five or more skills they have (good with social media, sewing, baking, good with grammar, spell well, have competency in more than one language, can do math problems quickly, etc.). Translating these skills into creating jobs is covered in the next section (Economic Awareness).

6. Invite people with interesting jobs that require certification or on-the-job training, such as cosmetologists, barbers, farmers, and store workers, among others, to come speak at "brown-bag" lunch dates to share their experiences with students. After the visits, create posters about job requirements and how to apply for such positions.

Economic Awareness

7. The U.S. Department of Treasury offers an interesting math curriculum, "Money Math: Lessons for Life" (https://www.treasurydirect.gov/indiv/tools/tools_moneymath.htm), that you can suggest to their math teachers; it is adaptable downward to grades 5–6 as well as allows you to add your ideas for library activities. These lessons cover topics such as "the secret to becoming a millionaire," measuring, budgeting, and taxes. The lesson on measuring is about how to measure walls for wallpaper. In the library, you could offer a series of lunchtime workshops on "redoing your room" and incorporate this math into the workshops as students go home and measure their own walls. Returning, you might help them meet a designer or suggest someone they could visit who would help them figure out how to decide on colors, wallpaper, or other design elements. Another workshop would cover budgeting and saving money. This offers the possibility to then offer workshops on finding jobs that they can do, such as mowing lawns and feeding/walking dogs, to make money.

Offer a workshop on building your business. Invite speakers from the local SCORE organization (https://www.score.org) to help students design their business cards and then print them out in the library for their babysitting, gardening, personal shopping, and similar businesses.

Students of this age should be interested in volunteering. If you have the young adult librarian from the nearest public library come to the school, students can volunteer to help with programs in the library such as children's storytime. If they do this job well, they may be able to apply for a job as a "page."

Have students take their skills they have identified from Activity 5 (Teacher-Directed Activities: https://www.msjc.edu/cte/Documents/MWTW-Teacher-Directed-Activities%20MSJC.pdf), mentioned earlier, for example, good with social media and so on, and have them join groups of other students with complementary skills that could lead to starting a business. "Complementary" might imply math skills align with a ballerina, a person with social media skills and a musician to start a dance studio, experts in gardening can start a gardening business while adding someone who is an organizer, and an artist and a math person could open a landscaping business. Students with dual languages and good science and math competencies could set up a tutoring business. All they need to do is to think creatively and out of the box.

8. Calculating credit card debt is an excellent math problem for students in junior high. Work with the math teacher to set up some scenarios such as the next two, or you can have your students create their own scenarios.

   Scenario 1. A credit card ad arrives in the mail. The insert promises there is no charge for the purchase of this card for one year. The first two months have 0 percent introductory annual percentage rate (APR). After that, this amount may vary as 14.94, 19.94, or 24.94 percent based on your credit worthiness and with the market based on the prime rate. It goes on to describe cash advances and paying interest. It also suggests that your cash advances will be 3 percent of each cash advance or $10, whichever is greater, and the amount of penalty fees if you fail to make a payment on time.

   Scenario 2. Credit card companies anticipate payment of the charges on bill when it is mailed. The company lists a minimum payment and the full amount of the charges. If you buy something that costs $100, the minimum payment on the bill is $10. Paying only $10 leaves a remainder of $90, and an 18 percent interest charge will be made so that the next total bill will be $90 + $16.70 = $106.70. It does not take long to see that credit card debt is crippling.

   Students can place other credit card purchases into this or the amounts charged by the credit card companies located in Scenario 1 to get a perspective on the cost of credit card debt.

9. Many junior high schools have clubs in place. Topics for library clubs often center on activities that are helpful in the management of the library, but this club should also include books and reading, which engages readers in a good way. Engage them in selecting resources by having them read reviews and create buying lists. If at all possible, have them review actual books and resources to make those selections.

   You might also consider a school literary magazine to highlight the best papers from classrooms. It could also include poetry and stories submitted by students. It is a good time to feature an entry from a student who may not be a top student but one who has given the best effort to the project.

   Organizing a totally different club could be helpful in these times. It should involve administration and the other teachers. Students who are interested in activism will need guidance to turn their enthusiasm into useful directions. Check for possible leaders in this

group to help you start. To create an activist group, see the recommendations from www
.tolerance.org. They offer excellent guidelines on starting a club at https://www.tolerance
.org/professional-development/starting-an-activist-club-at-school.

For students who are interested in protecting animals, the American Humane
Society offers advice on how to start an animal protection club at http://www
.humanesociety.org/about/departments/students/clubs/how_to_start_a_club.html.

10. Offer a parent/student civics night at the library, playing the "democracy challenge"
using iCivics.org. Through the use of apps and website games, families play games
such as "Counties Work," "Do I Have a Right," and "Branches of Power." These
games offer kick-start conversations about government and open conversations
between parents and their children. Offer dessert and provide discussion breaks as
you go along. Learn together and see how many problems can be solved through
collaboration, discussion, and open minds: https://www.icivics.org/democracyatplay
-family. *Note:* If an evening event does not work, try offering one at lunch for students
who will work together and have discussions along the way.

11. Visit a school board meeting and/or make a presentation at a school board meeting.
Have students help you show off what happens in the library. Raise any concerns
you may have with the school board after you have shown positive outcomes.

12. Visit a state legislator or your local congressional representative in his or her office or
ask this person to visit your school. It will be much easier to get a state legislator than
your congressional representative, but the latter is not an impossibility. To arrange a
visit to the office, locate the person's webpage and find the name of the "scheduler."
The scheduler will want to know who and how many are coming. If this includes
students, you will need to let them know about the accompanying adults who are to
come and the reason for the visit. Arranging to go to the office is much easier than
getting a legislator or your congressional representative to come to your school, but,
you will have no guarantee that your group will see the person or an aide because their
schedules change abruptly.

To arrange for a legislator to come to your school, you need to involve the school
district administration because such an action may affect activities about which you
are not aware. It will involve the entire school, so you need to get teachers interested
in the event. If all these are in agreement, the web page should have a heading
"Arrange a Visit" or similar title. If you do not find this information, again call your
legislator's local office and ask to speak with someone who can arrange a visit to your
school or to arrange a class visit to the office. This will most likely need to be done
months in advance, so plan ahead if you would like it to coincide with a planned event.
Often, legislators will send an aide if he or she cannot make it, so try to arrange it early
but anticipate the possibility the person will be called away to return to the office.
Once you have a visit arranged, you and your students need to consider what this

person should see featured throughout the building. Will you have posters with information, welcome signs, banners, lists of accomplishments? Will this guest address the entire school? Be sure to prep your students by helping them to ask questions. You may wish to use the QFT process as described in Chapter 2, Activity 7. Using the QFT process from rightquestion.org can be accomplished by learning the process from their website or their book: *Make Just One Change*. This simple step-by-step process teaches students to brainstorm the questions that occur to them and then gives them a process for identifying them, prioritizing them, and allowing them to decide which question they want to know most about. This activity will give students an opportunity to follow up with thank-you notes.

13. Make sure that all students know the "Presidents Song" on YouTube.com by playing it in the library. See https://knowledgequest.aasl.org/you-want-me-to-remember-what/ for how knowing this song helped a person get a job.

14. With the music teacher, introduce John Philip Sousa and his marching band music to students. Place his life in the historical events that were occurring when he composed those songs and where they are often played today. Students who watch parades such as Macy's Thanksgiving Day Parade and the Rose Parade can be asked to see if they can identify the songs played by the bands marching in those parades. Have a prize for the student who had the first accurate list. You may need to enlist someone from your music department to help you with this project if you are not familiar with marches.

15. Take some time to look at the website ICIVICS (icivics.org). Founded by Sandra Day O'Connor, teachers have access to hands-on lessons that can be followed up with games and other suggestions for active civics learning.

16. Do you want to encourage student activists? Check out Civic Action Project (CAP) from the Constitutional Rights Foundation (http://www.crfcap.org/mod/page/view.php?id=206). Use models from other schools and then sign up your class, club, or library assistants and create your own local advocacy project.

Notes

1. https://nurtureandthriveblog.com/the-surprising-reason-your-child-is-suddenly-cranky-and-what-to-do-about-it/.
2. Personal e-mail.
3. Personal e-mail.
4. "Data Point: Early High School Dropouts: What Are Their Characteristics?" U.S. Department of Education, February 2015, http://nces.ed.gov/surveys/hsls09.
5. Ibid.
6. https://bensguide.gpo.gov/.

Chapter 5

Reaching Out to High School Students, Grades 9–10

Students entering high school begin that last stretch of road with graduation just around the bend. They again move from the top of the ladder in junior high to low on the totem pole in high school. Many towns and cities have only one or two high schools, each with large student populations. This can mean that students from several junior high schools will discover that getting to school from different directions and distances becomes a challenge. Just as in junior high, students in high school come from many schools, and again, they may find themselves in classes where most, if not all, of the students are new to them. Finding new friends will be a challenge, and keeping old ones close can be a difficult process. This is another fork in the road for friendships as students entering high school discover an even larger student body and diverse activities to explore.

Their time here will be less directed by their teacher than in earlier grades, with greater expectations for homework completion, attention, and participation in class. In high school, increased choices for extracurricular activities mean facing new challenges with competition for spots on the many sports teams, the cheerleading squad, music, drama, and in other activities. Even when they are admitted as members of that sport or activity, it seems that competition is inherent as they compete for that A-team in soccer, first chair in the band, or lead in the school play.

Students may also form new groups that meet every day during lunch hour, providing a new family-like atmosphere, which supplies a social group for acceptance.

The very large elephant in the room for students starting ninth grade is that 2.7 percent will have dropped out by the time they should be juniors.[1] As discussed in Chapter 4, dropouts in this study are considered students who were not enrolled or had not completed high school or an alternative program by the 2012 interview. Race is a factor in these dropout rates, with the highest two being Hispanic and Black. This disparity continues the divide for those who end up looking for low-wage jobs. While it is hoped that these students have been identified by junior high and some remediation is underway, catching these students and working with them one-on-one is imperative as they enter high school.

High schools have many different approaches to helping these at-risk students, and the library can be a big part of those solutions. Working as part of the academic team with counselors, special education teachers, and English as a second language (ESL) teachers, you can provide support for these students by ensuring that they as well as other students have access to the best information possible and the tools and skills they need. You will be showing them "the way to succeed." You are well placed to provide that big picture view for them to connect the dots that can be easily missed. It is major part of your responsibilities as a librarian.

Responsibilities for the School Librarian

You have an excellent opportunity to offer a familiar, welcoming spot for new students. They may not have been in your library before today, but they have been in a library, and if your doors are open and welcoming at the beginning of the school day where they can come to study and maybe meet old friends, you will remain an oasis, a safe haven, for their entire time in the school. Making sure that your collection, instruction, and programming show your students that they are all welcome there will go a long way to ensuring that students will feel comfortable in your library.

As stated earlier, students arriving at a new school combining several schools means new groups may form with only a few friends from their former junior high. While membership in these groups may change throughout the school years, "cliques" develop early on with certain lunch areas staked out for "jocks," "stoners," "nerds," and any other targeted named group. If this is true in your school, the library—at lunch—is often the "safe" space for those who feel that they do not belong anywhere.

Offering a safe haven during the lunch hour is an excellent time for you to offer compelling programming that crosses "clique" borders and entices many students to join a new group or at least to expand their friendships across group lines. Brown-bag lunches work just as well at high school as they did in the earlier grades, and you can continue to offer hands-on activities. The difference is the sophistication of the topics to be discussed. These lunches can feature something related to their classrooms too. This could be especially useful, and important for many students, if you are not collaborating with particular teachers and you know that you can offer resources and skill building through the library. Sometimes teachers see an interesting library activity and, with your invitation, might be willing to integrate it into their curriculum next time.

Collaborating with teachers can bring the classroom into the library at lunch by offering things like one librarian's "MAD" Wednesday. As a high school librarian in Hollister, California, Doug Achterman offered a program, MAD Wednesday: Music, Art, Drama. Students shared the makeshift stage to put on musical shows, improvisations, and art activities. A successful activity at one of the author's high schools was the invitation to a local makeup artist to come in and show students how to do a makeup "makeover." Another was makeup advice from local clinicians and dress shops. These are the extra opportunities that can add value to your students' lives by extending their interests beyond the school walls. These will lead students to be interested in your instructional role.

Your instructional role may vary with whether students have had a professional school librarian in their previous schools. Information literacy instruction is key here. If there are no school librarians in the elementary or junior high schools in your district, then you are the door that opens for them to become information-literate students. Working to create collaborations with teachers is important at ninth grade so that students can get a good start to their high school years. Even if they come from schools with excellent school librarians, many will have forgotten many skills over the summer.

Starting with ninth-grade orientation, these students will discover that you offer information and materials they need for their classes even as the great, vast Internet beckons for easy answers. Orientation is an excellent time to gather a picture of who your students are when they are in the library for that freshman orientation.

The first orientation can offer a tour of the library to introduce your services, what is there and where to find things, the hours of operation, and how to access materials and the library website, the nuts and bolts of library rules and regulations. Should your school be a 1:1 school, they will need to set up their device with library resources residing on their home screen or prominently on the school's learning management system, an excellent use of this time. Be sure to make it as much "hands-on" as possible because just showing and talking about something means those words of wisdom may be lost when they leave the library.

What information students can access from their homes may be all you can cover in the time allotted for this, keeping in mind that most of the information you are giving will need to be repeated again and again. You will let them know that you will be available to help them find the information they need when they can come to the library and that you will be working with their teachers when assignments are underway.

If a little time is available, perhaps the guidance counselor could be invited to point out how to change any courses that might be different if those were chosen at the end of the eighth grade. This cooperation with the guidance counselor will point out your availability to help them with any challenges they might encounter during these first few weeks and throughout their high school.

Orientation is a good time to try to find students who will want to be helpful in the library, those who might be interested in service credit or worked in their junior high libraries and wish to continue. Identifying those interested in technology can become a tech squad for you both in the library and in their classrooms, thus saving your time and effort helping teachers with minor technical problems. This is the year to get them to sign up so they can fit it into any other activities they may be choosing, such as band, chorus, the improv group, or the debate team. Your tech squad members who have worked with you for the previous years will be able to help train these initiates with what they have learned and what they do.

Community-service requirements generally start in the ninth grade. You can invite as many as possible to earn these in your library. Depending upon the type of credit and length of time to gain those points, you can decide which jobs you want the students to carry out for you. While they can easily shelve books, those tasks need to be moderated with things that would be more engaging, such as reading reviews of new materials, creating lists for potential orders for new items, or creating a display case. Providing your community-service students with a targeted task, such as "create bookmarks with genre titles on them" or "prepare a presentation on how to use our databases to put online," will not only help you get the word out about the library and its services but also give those students opportunities to connect the library to their peers.

What happens with students and the library after orientation is dependent upon your relationship with your teachers. Collaboration with teachers provides you the opportunity to continue helping students become proficient with the many literacies they need to master. If you are not sure your teachers understand what you have available to offer to their students, you can provide the professional development your faculty may need through the different ways that professional development is provided in your school. This can include the formal professional development day-long presentations when schools are closed to students, or the every-day-in-the-hall request to collaborate, or your offer to drop in on a class with a project underway and you are needed to teach an information literacy skill.

Helping teachers with guided-inquiry assignments in the actual classroom will let students know you are a part of their learning teams. This is an especially good time to try to get teachers creating lessons with inquiry in mind; hopefully you can use these connections to set the stage for schoolwide inquiry instruction.

Many teachers may be teaching to pass state or national tests, and this most often means that teachers pay less attention to the kind of research and writing that requires the librarian. One can feel the sense of isolation when teachers no longer spend time teaching through inquiry or assign more traditional reports with limited need to conduct research. This greatly reduces the opportunity for students to come to the library. Teaching to the test seldom bases any curriculum in something students recognize as learning for life. It takes a very assertive librarian with good suggestions and collegial connections to make inroads into the classes to help make the coursework interesting and to help place what they are learning in the context of what students need to prepare for life after high school as well as passing the tests required by any agency. Yet, if you do not try, it will not happen. This is doable but frustrating and difficult. Finding classroom colleagues who can be allies in this quest will confirm your value to the learning process and perhaps be the catalyst to full collaboration.

Because teaching to the test is pervasive throughout the country, in this book programming is suggested for you as an opportunity to offer outside of class activities to students to help them make "real-life" connections. Many students will be interested in participating when you help them see how these activities connect to successfully planning for their future after high school. With active advocacy and interesting programming, you may find that teachers begin to incorporate this information into their classrooms. At the very least, you can see if teachers will give "extra credit" for time spent with library activities related to these issues.

For those students who have that sixteenth birthday, even more challenges await them. Age 16 is an important milestone for many reasons, but foremost in most students' minds is the fact that they are eligible to take the test for their driver's licenses. What a myriad of life choices this takes: What will they drive? How much will their parents' insurance costs increase? Will they drive their parents' car, or do they need to make enough money to purchase a car, pay for insurance, and take on any other costs as needed? Are they mature enough to have the responsibility of driving? Are they ready to follow all the rules of the road? Helping students understand this along with a healthy amount of caution about this responsibility may echo what they are hearing at home.

Age 16 also allows students to think seriously about their future and the role of school. If they are already having a difficult time, they may be considering dropping out. Leaving school without a plan creates difficulties that can follow them throughout their lives. Those for whom school is important and who, while they might not have a clear vision of their future, believe that school is an important vehicle to sorting it all out will be considering which classes to take and how to make the most of their remaining school years.

At the high school level, standards like the C3 Social Studies Framework place their expected accomplishments by grade blocks rather than single grades. This means that instead of knowing that grade 9 will cover one area of the content standard, it can be covered in several grade levels. These are usually skills-based content standards so that learning, for example, how to provide evidence to a claim is covered in ninth grade, and it can also be covered in tenth and eleventh grades, with competency shown in the twelfth grade. If your school follows this format, it works well for you to offer programming that can reach a wide audience from all the grades. Thus, younger students will learn some new skills, and older students can take away information that they will be using right away or soon after high school. A major challenge is the information needed but seldom taught in the classroom: how to find employment.

Hosting events such as job fairs and speakers and creating an information board about internships or volunteer opportunities for this level of high school can bring students into the library throughout the school day and from all grade levels. Work with your counselors or career center personnel to locate important dates for students to learn as much as possible about places to gain experience and perhaps earn a salary while they are still in high school.

The Education Environment

The educational environment in high schools varies across the country. Days may be divided into class periods all the same length, following the same schedule day after day. They may also be blocked into longer classes and on alternate days. Some schools have adopted a school day when no bells ring to indicate the end of a class, making it the students' responsibility to move between classes. Some schools offer long blocks of time where students study one or two subjects for a longer period of time and then rotate to another set for the next few weeks. As in all of education, there is much conversation about how to best educate our children, and many schools are willing to give new trends a try, including later start times and creative scheduling.

Longer class periods are certainly better for you because you can fit more easily into the curriculum with library and classroom visits that have enough time to be meaningful. Successful collaborations have included coteaching throughout a unit of study, and the longer periods allow for that sort of transition. Carefully reviewing the content of the unit of study may provide you with a means to add something that will bring the students to the library for an activity related to life after high school.

Libraries in schools that have study halls for students who are not in extracurricular activities or who take fewer classes can be open for those students to complete their homework or help out in the library. Providing interesting educational experiences for students who have completed their assignments gives them an opportunity to investigate training or education opportunities for them now or in the immediate future.

> Because study-hall periods by necessity need to be quiet, activities for those who are not engaged in studying probably should be quiet. Here is where a library website can add to learning while offering interesting learning experiences through gaming or other web-based activities. If budget allows, having a career database, some interesting games, a language-based course, and magazine subscriptions can offer quiet, yet learning-directed, activities. If there is no budget, there are free choices available. Curating these can be the job of a library helper with oversight from you.

Student placement in high school classes may come from their previous teachers who have analyzed the students' performances, test scores, and parental input. Some parents may have very strong ideas about just what and where their children will go after that last high school class, and they will be proactive in making sure their children have the courses that will get them there. Decisions about placement should be a collaborative one that includes the students, counselors, parents, and teachers. When that is not the situation, students may not understand the framework they need to establish in ninth grade. In this first year of high school, students generally take a set of course core classes, a physical education class, and possibly an elective, often a foreign language. If your school offers other courses such as a "wheel" including health or other short courses, then your students may have the opportunity to pick an elective of their choice, such as music or art. While some students may have a general idea of what they might like to do, most do not, especially at this beginning. As stated earlier, making sure that all students know and understand the many course opportunities allotted to them could be tied to your orientation sessions.

Guidance counselors may also have a general career-orientation program for all the students that is offered throughout the ninth-grade school year. It is designed to help guide students as they are able to choose more of their classes over the coming years. Because a single library-orientation or career-guidance session is not an effective way to help students understand how to improve their research skills, manage their time, and develop the other skills needed as high school students, your library programming in collaboration with counselors can assist with providing activities that help students understand the process of choosing classes as well as those activities that bring them into the library to practice skills they are learning in class. You can help guidance counselors identify any students you see who are confused about their classes and their class schedules and, at the same time, be aware of how to fit this into the need to choose a career, become financially literate, and accept the responsibilities of citizenship.

For those students who seem to fit the description of those who might not finish high school, you and the guidance counselor can share efforts to provide information about the

General Equivalency Diploma (GED) or other high school equivalency tests mentioned in Chapter 1 as well as alternative schools, internships, or other possibilities so that the student leaves with a positive goal. Community college can be a possible next step for these students, so you support the counselor with connections to those resources. Community-college counselors can be invited to come to the library to explain any services or opportunities students might have to sign up for classes. The opportunity for students to return to training at a later time is easier for the student who has thought through the many options available. Public libraries are offering high school diploma courses also through the Career Online High School for those who did not graduate high school and are determined to return to get a diploma (http://www.careeronlinehs.gale.com/).

Those students who are college bound need to begin that preparation. Some may have already started by taking foreign language or algebra in junior high and will continue with these throughout high school. Others will stick with the process that only meets graduation requirements. In some states, there are also high school graduation requirements that are specific to college entrance. In California, for example, the A-G schedule of classes that include stepped-up courses through the grades creates the preparation for college that can make for easier acceptance. Some schools are converting all their courses to A-G with much dissent because such a move can create a larger pool of dropouts because it does not allow time in the schedule for vocational or other elective courses. There is much discussion to be had on these issues.

Preparation for that college-application process begins here in the ninth grade with the counselor and parent discussion of goals for the high school year. Any college discussion also includes the requirement for a resume including community service and extracurricular activities. The importance of a record of participation in extracurricular activities during the school year is needed. College admission committees look for the types of activities and the level of leadership within those clubs and on those teams.

College admission requirements are also going through many changes, with some dropping the essay requirement and others thinking about following suit. While admissions policies may change, they will continue to look for students who are ready to move forward socially and intellectually and with a curiosity for learning. Continuing to teach critical thinking and inquiry, encouraging wide reading, and creating lifelong learners will always be important attributes higher education will seek in their new admissions. You and other librarians can foster these throughout your work with teachers and students in instruction and programming.

Students with their families will hopefully begin to work through the myriad of decisions about their education and choose what types of classes they would like to take in order to reach their educational goal. Students have many opportunities to take a risk and step out of their comfort zone to enroll in an elective about something they know little and have little experience. It is not unusual for students to discover a passion within a class that changes everything. Students learn that the Advanced Placement (AP) courses, while perhaps more work than other classes, help them start college with credits already collected, thus saving tuition for a similar course, or allow them to take another elective they would enjoy. Some community colleges allow students to take classes while they are still in high school. Any other opportunities such as online courses offered through the school can make up for any missing opportunities along the way. You have a role to provide the resources they need to be good taking tests.

You can continue to offer resources that help, such as testing books available to practice the SAT, ASVAB, and ACT, among others, as well as books and databases about careers, biographies, and fiction that show the many options available. With the guidance counselor, make sure you have as many online resources as possible to research all kinds of training available for students as well as colleges and universities: the application process, their entrance requirements, tuition and housing costs, scholarships offered, size of the campus, and degrees offered, among others. What they can find out at the beginning of high school can help them with courses to take and even how to start earning money for further education after high school.

The Career Environment

You and your guidance counselors, working together with teachers at this level, begin to focus directly on students in their preparation for life after high school. Including parents whenever possible in the discussions will encourage a team approach to helping students understand that there are many choices they can make about their lives. You can offer opportunities for parents to gain insight through speaker evenings perhaps given before open house or back-to-school night 📝 or other already established school evening events. These are particularly important for low-income parents and caregivers who need to learn of opportunities for students both in school and out of school because they may not have had such opportunities themselves. Community-service hours and learning job-preparation skills will be some of the activities to report during these speaker evenings.

Many high school librarians organize programs to give their students opportunities to choose their careers with their teachers and guidance counselors. When it involves the local business people and other community members, it draws them into the school activities and shows them the role of the school librarian in student learning.

You can also create templates, preferably electronically, for students to use to document their community-service hours 📝 and hold resume-writing workshops, as well as hosting speakers to come in, much as they did in junior high to offer job fairs, interviewing practice, and other skill-building activities. Some who attended these in junior high

Leslie Poston, librarian at the Kiski School, an all-boys school in Saltsburg, Pennsylvania, reports, "Our tenth graders all take a semester of Health and Wellness and a semester of Ethics, which we call Men in Society. I collaborate with the teachers to do a unit of career exploration and preparation. This includes personality assessments, career research, along with resume and cover letter writing. Time permitting, we also cover payroll taxes and employee benefits. For the culminating activity, we invite a dozen or so local business people and community members to come and conduct mock interviews for each student. They are graded on poise, presentation and professionalism. Our students take it pretty seriously, because these persons aren't just teachers interviewing them."

may not have felt that it applied to them then, and it might not have. Here in high school, however, getting a job is a real possibility for many students, and gaining information at workshops like these helps them to understand the process of getting hired. Some may still be too young for retail or other standard jobs, but as students move toward and into tenth grade, these jobs can become available to them.

Documenting their service hours as well as keeping a record of their activities that might go on a resume begin here and are added to throughout high school. Is the service experience going to be something that will give them a reference for the next service experience or internship they might apply for two years ahead?

One thing to consider adding to a community-service log is a box for students to include skills they used on the job, using active verbs. Examples include *speaking* to customers, *keeping patient* with young children, *organizing* books, and *logging* feeding times. These active verbs will be helpful to these students when they begin to think about resumes. Many businesses today would like to know what skills applicants might bring to their job, and having a set of active skill words in their job application will be useful as they build their resumé.

While the search for a potential career continues, students are reaching the age when they can get a work permit. With the guidance counselor, this information is made available to students who may not have any information or may not have all the information. The laws for each state and perhaps within a city may vary, so you need to make sure you have the correct information for them.

When these students have their work permits, efforts begin to help students find part-time jobs during the school year and summer work experiences. For some students, this may be their way to continue their education after high school. For others, it may be the way to stay in high school when their earnings are a part of the family income. One of the conditions of having a work permit is an acceptable grade point average, and this may encourage students to keep up on their school work. A student with a paid job will have less time to cause trouble and less need to be in a gang-related situation. You can support these students by offering quiet spaces to complete homework and support as needed. The goal is to help these students finish high school.

Students begin practicing their skills for meeting strangers as they grow through the teen years. They are growing taller and looking more like an adult, and they will be expected to act like an adult. This includes understanding how to meet, greet, and engage with potential employers and colleagues as a professional equal. This kind of conversation begins with that opening statement that hopefully gains the interest of the person(s) conducting the interview. Practicing an "elevator speech" is a good way to start this.

Counselors begin to administer tests to help students turn the things they like to do into potential career choices. Find out from your guidance counselors what tests they administer, when, and what they do with the results. Some public libraries as well as your library host the databases that can be used for such tests and profile building. Before the guidance counselor begins administering these tests, you can post a short introduction to the resources available in the library to help them prepare for these tests throughout the school and on the library website. When the counselors go to classrooms to administer these tests, your library is a great place to bring out those career books, build displays of possible careers, and offer speakers.

As stated earlier, this is not easy in a teach-to-the-test environment when what students are being given for study and testing seems totally unrelated to what they need to find and hold a job. Your library can be a place where bulletin boards and displays encourage students to continue to study. Flyers, databases, and folders, with information about occupations and the pay scale with the needed education to be eligible for that job, are something that students can research, perhaps as a part of that "service learning" they may be doing.

Economic Environment

Because financial literacy is not a core subject in most schools, this creates an opportunity for you to offer programming that opens the doors to many of the concepts needed to take care of money. Building on the skills that could be introduced in the junior high, burgeoning workers in retail, agriculture, industry, or offices can benefit from on-site-at-the-library programs that help them to manage money and plan on how they can earn and save toward future goals, such as college, travel, or apartment living. Some ninth- and tenth-grade math teachers enjoy teaching units about "real life," providing an excellent opportunity to coteach skills such as researching the cost of an apartment. Creating learning stations in the library with practical application is a fun way to let students know that they use math every day. 🗐

Many news programs carry news of the status of the stock market: which indicator went up or down. Sometimes these even give reports of the international stock market. Students who might be interested in this will probably study it in an economics class in their last two years, but if they are interested at this time, you may provide an opportunity for them to do this in the library. 🗐

It is not too early for students who want to continue in a training program or further education after high school to begin to assess how that cost fits into their finances. They will need to tabulate the probable cost for all those items they have been looking up as a part of their career planning. How much will it likely cost to take that training or attend that academic program? If they borrow from a bank, what interest is charged, and how does one calculate that? If they should get a job during high school or even wait to attend college until they can save money, how long might this take? 🗐

While most high school students will not be employed full-time with benefits that mean they have taxes taken out of their paychecks, they can begin to understand the impact of taxes on their lives. Questions to include in discussions are as follows: What taxes are placed on gasoline and why? How much do gasoline taxes vary from state to state and why? What do property taxes in your states cover? 🗐 Paying taxes is a part of an adult's civic responsibility as well as their financial obligation. The next section covers a student's role in government: local, state, and national.

Civic Responsibility

Students who have been given an opportunity to learn about their local, state, and national governments in their earlier grades can begin to put their knowledge into action. Not all students may have been given this background, so your civics teachers can give you some help in finding charts to display the relationship between the president, the Supreme Court, and Congress, how a bill is passed, and a copy of the Bill of Rights, among others. Creating activities that include basic information about the governance at local, state, and national level can help those students catch up on anything they may have missed. 🗐

Helping the entire school have more opportunities for interaction with elected officials begins with these students and continues throughout their four years. The election process can start with a lunchtime discussion with interested students who bring their brown-bag lunches to the library. 🗐

Students who have been volunteering or are assigned for service learning in their school library, office, or classrooms might begin to now go outside the school to expand their service and offer their skills as a volunteer. Throughout the school year and in the summers, students may be able to volunteer for experiences helping in such places as a hospital, senior center, or animal shelter, bettering the lives of those who are there. Some students may have the opportunity to visit another country for several weeks with their religious or other club to help repair local buildings or participate in other projects. You can post and advertise opportunities that are available for those who might be interested.

During election season, a student who is interested in helping a candidate can contact the headquarters of the political party or the candidate to find out what could be done. Library bulletin boards can display a list of local campaign headquarters from all parties and help students connect with them. It would be an appropriate time to have a legislator come to the school for a brown-bag lunch.

The amount of publicity placed during elections can lead to many research activities, such as an analysis of whom a particular television ad is focused to attract. It may cover other aspects of the cost to a candidate for election.

As mentioned in Chapter 2, the elementary chapter, "makercare" is an alternative way to incorporate the sense of "maker" with caring for others, civics, and entrepreneurship. Creating objects that are needed by others is a way that the library can offer community engagement right there at school. Gina Seymour's *Makers with a Cause: Creative Service Projects for Library Youth* (Santa Barbara, CA: Libraries Unlimited, 2018) has many helpful ideas.

The mechanisms in place to choose leaders begin in earnest in high school. Class, student-council, and club leaders are chosen early in each school year. When the school allows for campaigning for these offices, the library can be a go-to place to work on posters and other things for this part of the high school career.

In some locations, students can be chosen to serve on the school board and public library boards or even represent students in city government. Help students locate this information through bulletin board or morning announcements. If you know of students who you think might serve well, seek them and encourage them to apply. Many students who thought they had nothing to offer find that they do, indeed, have something; a personal nudge from you can make a big difference in their confidence. While these may seem to be more applicable to the next two grades, they can be thinking about it now.

This chapter has covered those first two years of high school. Attention is given to choices of courses for the high school to prepare them for the next steps. The next chapter covers what will happen in those last two years.

Suggested Activities

Responsibilities for the Librarian

1. During the first weeks of the school year, you can offer the opportunity for students to bring their lunches to the library. Many students may be eager to get out of the noise and chaos of the school cafeteria and come eagerly no matter the topic. At the beginning, you may need to create the topics such as sharing new books in the library. As the semester progresses, you can establish a committee of those students who come regularly to allow them to help suggest topics and even find speakers to come to the school.

2. Orientation for new students to the high school gives an opportunity for them to provide you with information to allow you to help as they continue through high school. Create a Google form or any other online form and ask pertinent questions about their course schedules, hobbies, and reading and recreation interests. Ask the questions that help you understand their academic goals, and you can use the information to plan purchases; it is also a way for you to informally touch base with students you might not normally see. They will do this if you explain that it is to help you help them when they need information, and you will expect them to help you by updating this database each semester. You will need their name, homeroom, planned course of study, a favorite book or author, and what they like to do in their leisure time. Knowing that playing computer games might be the most often chosen from any list of activities, be sure to ask the names and nature of games they like. This will help you understand current teenage trends as well as possible ideas for future activities. Having this information for you to refer to easily will help you get acquainted with students as they come into the library. One final question might have to do with their plans after high school. Some may already be planning to attend a training course or a college. If you are not sure what to ask on this list, a group of your student library workers can help with these choice items.

3. Developing a geek squad to help in your library is discussed in the activities section of previous chapters. The difference here is that students may be even better prepared to take on this role in the school, saving you even more time. They can also train other students less skillful if they want to participate. It is an excellent opportunity for students to serve their school and get valuable experience. Often these groups form into other tech activities, including filmmaking, podcasting, or other techie things.

4. The "usual suspects" for student helpers' tasks include shelving, inventory, locating lost books, and creating bulletin boards or building displays. Thinking out of the box means that you consider some larger goals that help promote library resources while teaching a transferable skill to other venues and content areas. Brainstorming ways to promote library services with your student staff can bring interesting and even

quirky ideas. Ask them to create "We Can Help" brochures with social service agencies and leave them scattered around campus. Ask them to create a library logo and "brand" and add it to all publicity and instructional materials. Then assign the task of marketing the brand. Not only will this market your brand and provide a service for the library but it will also teach marketable skills. Locating a need in town or a charity that fits in with your library culture, ask helpers to organize a fund-raiser and follow through with the charity.

Education Environment

5. At your brown-bag lunches, invite the guidance counselor to join you in talking with students about the information they should maintain in preparation with that college entrance application. Create an electronic spreadsheet that they can add to or revise easily. Some divisions might include the lists of their honors and extracurricular activities both in school and in other activities, such as Boy and Girl Scouts. This could include "volunteering," or that could be a separate column. A separate form to record community-service hours is discussed in the next activity. Whom they might choose to write letters of reference is another column. Finally, they will need to prepare a resume. This is covered in the next chapter where a sample document to fill in is provided.

Career Information

6. Check out the other chapters about creating a school library presence at back-to-school night or offering an open house. It will be more of a challenge to get parents to come to school at a time other than when they come to talk with their teachers at an evening event, but if the topic is important enough that students will want to bring their parents, it will be a success. One might also count such an event successful even if only one or two parents who need the information attend.

    Having speakers come to school to speak has been suggested in previous chapters. Here in the ninth grade, these opportunities have more application to real life than they have had in the past. Plan these well, and your audience will arrive.

7. If your school does not have a form to collect this information, a template to record community-service hours might be as follows:

Dates	Agency	Supervisor	Activities Accomplishments	Comments

8. Elevator speeches are excellent ways to "capture" someone and convince them about something. Help students identify their passion, skills, and/or goals so that if given the

chance, they could wow someone within a few short sentences. Their assignment: "If you have 15 floors to capture attention on why you are a fit for this organization or job, you would say: . . . ." Have them write it up and then calculate how many minutes they took to leave that fabulous, lasting impression. Help them prepare by making a list:

Company: (What it does)	Company: (Goals/mission)	Student: (Personal qualities and goals)	Student: (Experience and/or skills)

9. This display should have very up-to-date information about careers. It is time to have your student assistants share a list of the database trial tests you own for students to gain confidence in test taking and any information about similar tests at the public library. These students could demonstrate the databases of college catalogs from those surrounding your library.

Economic Awareness

10. https://www.imaginelearning.com/blog/2017/04/math-real-life-examples. Developing learning stations has been discussed in previous chapters. This website offers challenges that can be a fun way to introduce the thought that "we use math every day." While these would be best presented within a classroom context, they can also be a fun "corner stop" learning center for students to challenge themselves during an off-period time, such as lunch or before/after school.

11. For those students who love math challenges, the following may help them begin mastering the variables of the stock market. For those to whom such things seem foreign, these games work just as well, helping them to unravel the mysteries through game activities.

   • Student Stock Trader: http://studentstocktrader.com/

   • Stock Market Game: https://www.stockmarketgame.org/

   • How the Market Works: http://www.howthemarketworks.com/

   Review each of these or others online. You should try it yourself and see how you do; you can then offer library contests or other fun activities. Create a discussion group to talk about what works, what does not, and whether luck comes into play or if it is all about strategy.

12. A template to focus on costs of training or college is shown here:

Institution	Tuition	Housing	Books	Other	Subtotal	Debt	%	# of Years	Grand Total

13. USA.gov offers an excellent lesson plan on taxes. While this might seem to be only useful for teachers in the classroom, ask if you can collaborate with them on this. You can also use some of these materials in the library, especially during election season or just before taxes due day, usually, but not always, April 15, depending on what day of the week April 15 falls (https://www.usa.gov/taxes-lesson-plan).

    To adapt it to the library through an interactive bulletin board, do the following:

    a. Write the word "Taxes" on the board. Underneath it write, "What questions do you have about taxes?" Leave it up for a week or so and encourage students to write their questions. Engage teachers in this also and ask them to add their questions.

    b. Hold a "tax day" at lunch in the library with some math activities relating to taxes.

    c. Invite a panel of speakers on the subject. If your city is floating a tax raise in the upcoming election or if there is controversy about taxes locally, invite speakers to speak directly on this subject.

Civic Responsibility

14. Have your library helpers gather information and create bulletin boards with information about our local, state, and national governance; how bills are created and passed; who can run for president of the United States, Congress; and who can serve on the Supreme Court. They can create question-and-answer quizzes for students who come into the library and want to test their knowledge of the governance structure of where they live.

    Think about the many ways that the top U.S. 100 documents (https://www.ourdocuments.gov/content.php?flash=true&page=milestone) can be used in the library. Challenge students to place the documents on a timeline in the library by date, organizing by topic, era, or effect on our lives today. Post a scavenger hunt or questions to be answered on the library door.

15. Tamara Cox, librarian at Wren High School, Piedmont, South Carolina, helps her students become politically aware and engaged in being a good citizen. When it is time for students to vote on their state book award, she invites their county's voting commission to their school. They bring voting booths so that students can vote for their favorite book on a real voting machine. This information is expanded in the next chapter.

16. Plan a brown-bag lunch and invite someone who has worked during an election to tell students how to go about volunteering for a candidate and what they might be asked to do. The speaker should be cautioned that this is an information-gathering session and not a political event so that talking about any particular candidate or party is not allowed on campus. If there is an upcoming election, and the speaker can hand out information about the specifics of helping at the polls, among others, that would be even better. The League of Women Voters is one organization that can come to

schools and explain how supporting a candidate through activities like making calls to prospective voters with a prepared speech will help a student learn to talk to people and find out what it is to have a negative call as well as an affirmative call. Each campaign has its own rules about age limits, among other things, but many students work side by side with their parents on election-volunteer activities, and it might be another way your students can get community-service hours while providing an excellent look into how our election process works. Youth.gov is a government website that features ideas that you can use within your own community to create highly effective youth programs that work. The tools you need to understand community needs and locate local information and funding are included.

17. A broader step is to invite a state or national legislator to come to the school. This will take the approval of the principal and perhaps the school board, and if this person is coming, it will generate a media event. Information about the guest will be displayed in the library. If this happens, there should be preparation for the students to properly meet and greet this dignitary and ask appropriate questions about issues that are coming up in the legislature. Students should be made aware of the Question Formulation Technique (QFT) process as described in Chapter 2, Activity 7. This process allows students to brainstorm appropriate questions to ask this guest. After developing their questions, the group can decide which questions they want to know most about and perhaps decide who will ask the question. A legislator's time will be short, and to have this question-and-answer time well thought out will help students have the information they want.

18. The cost of any candidate running for office in the present climate is difficult to calculate. However, students may analyze the effect they think television ads, newspaper reports, and even lawn posters and bumper stickers supporting a candidate have on the election. They can compare the ads of the different candidates and decide whether they are helpful to learn more about the candidate or are merely trying to tarnish the opposition. Researching all candidates to see if what they say they support is what happens after election is always an interesting study, although it is not one that can be finished quickly. If a candidate cannot fulfill the promises made, was there some reason this happened?

Suggested Resources for Further Information

Abilock, Debbie, Kristin Fontichiaro, and Violet H. Harada, eds. *Growing Schools: Librarians as Professional Developers*. Santa Barbara, CA: Libraries Unlimited, 2012.

Ehrenreich, Barbara. *Nickel and Dimed: On (Not) Getting By in America*. New York: Picador, 2011.

Klaus, Peggy. *Brag! The Art of Tooting Your Own Horn without Blowing It*. New York: Warner Business Books, 2003.

Kuhlthau, Carol C., Leslie K. Maniotes, and Ann K. Caspari. *Guided Inquiry Design: A Framework for Inquiry in Your School*. Santa Barbara, CA: Libraries Unlimited, 2012.

Note

1. "Data Point; U.S. Department of Education NCES 2015-066," February 2015, https://nces.ed.gov/pubs2015/2015066.pdf.

Chapter 6

Last Chances: Working with High School Students, Grades 11–12

The last two years of high school are truly the finishing touches on what has gone before and begin the march toward graduation. Life lessons started in elementary school, asking students to identify community helpers, and moved to junior high, where students began to think about their own identity and how they fit into their community and the larger world; these lessons are beginning to come together. While thinking about "what they want to be when they grow up," recognizing money denominations was used to begin financial literacy. The students have been introduced to their responsibilities as citizens in a democracy, learning the challenges they face as soon as they walk up to the graduation podium. Hopefully, they have mastered much of the information literacy lessons and can recognize when they have an information need, think through how to address it, and move forward to action.

The other skills that are the focus of this book—getting the education they need, choosing a career and how to obtain it, becoming financially literate, and becoming fully aware of the role of a citizen in a democracy—are hopefully ingrained into their own thinking routines. Those actions include introspection into how they might like to live their lives and how they will move into the community at large. Carlton Heywood, Teacher Librarian at Brashear High School in Pittsburgh, Pennsylvania, has the following suggestions from his experiences:

> One of the activities I started here at Brashear High School is the "Student Professional Development" series of workshops that are hosted and facilitated by students in the library. These go on throughout the year and are much akin to the mandatory Teacher Professional Development workshops that are offered districtwide. Our "Money Moves" workshop makes everyone take a hard look at teens and how they spend their money prompting saving and investing. Bank executives from a local bank came to speak, and library materials were displayed. Other workshops highlighted proper dress and attire improving proper dress and attire throughout the school, including faculty and staff, and led to some positive modification in student behavior. Our school proudly represents students from international backgrounds and different cultures. Our workshops proved to be beneficial as we learned from each other, and our teachers were appreciative and encouraging.

> A club that I sponsor, "The Future is Mine" club is designed for many students who feel unprepared for the transition and responsibilities that they need after 12th grade. We choose several topics and invite experts from several fields into the library and have down-to-earth, engaging discussions such as "Dress to Impress in the Workplace," "Resume Building," "Soft Skills," and my favorite, "Making Money Moves for Teens." Students must sign up for the lunch period discussions, and some teachers assign their classes to attend.

These last two years allow students to refine their goals and practices and improve those skills they have been learning for the past 10 years. Lessons and activities given in previous years provide them insights into finding resources, thinking about how to evaluate them, and then staking their claim backed up with evidence. These two years allow them to refine their skills.

Even those who are not going to make it to that diploma need to be reminded of the many possibilities available to them through adult school, the General Equivalency Diploma (GED), or other tests and programs. Help them make a connection to their next step choices. High school juniors face ever-increasing choices that have much greater impacts on their lives. If they were not 16 before the end of their sophomore year, they may be taking driver's education and face all those challenges mentioned in the previous chapter concerning the availability of a car to drive, the cost of maintaining that car, and the insurance costs to their parents. What will they drive? How will this affect the family budget with insurance increases?

One thing that is noticeable is the jump in maturity that students make during that summer of the year between the tenth and eleventh grades. The ability to get that driver's license is one. To choose what further training or education they will need, and in what school, and what all those choices might look like after graduation brings home a real feeling that there is a freedom coming their way while facing the responsibilities that go with it.

While there is no one path that all students should follow, each student should have the opportunity to learn about what the pros and cons could be for each choice.

Responsibilities for the School Librarian

These two years are your last opportunity to work with these already young adults to make sure that those skills are finely honed. While for some, of course, the library is not a big part of their school experience, all have gone through the doors, participated in some instruction and activities, and will hopefully remember the key points, among them the hope that they will remember the library as a place to take their children when they become parents. It is not too late for you to intervene. For any students who have been told that if they stay out of trouble and make passing grades they can have it all, you still have time to tell them how to achieve what they want to achieve.

You will concentrate on helping students understand the importance of becoming information literate and remaining lifelong learners. Because the role of social media in their lives is hugely prevalent, you can help them use this media effectively and responsibly; if not in class, then through programming and informal conversations throughout the day.

You can direct your programming and instruction to continue to help students gain the confidence they need to be able to locate, evaluate, create, and critically think through their information needs while helping them with those things that are necessary for them to accomplish in the required time frame. This is what you and the other librarians in your district have been aiming for your students from grade 1.

Learning how to manage time may become more difficult for these young adults who will be driving themselves to activities and perhaps helping parents get other siblings to their practices and games. They may be even busier with homework as teachers strive to have them ready for testing for college, and they hold down part-time jobs while participating in after-school activities, volunteer work, and family time. This is another area that is ripe for a library program: time-management workshops and speakers.

Remind students that, while you can help them identify career paths and possible careers, at this stage what they really need to know is that they will be facing a world where there might be jobs that have not been invented yet, so what they need are skills that transfer across many broad areas: critical thinking, inventiveness, collaboration skills, and resourcefulness, which exist alongside factual knowledge of math, language arts, history, and science.

While most students in your school will have gone through career planning in the ninth or tenth grade, interests change, and because very few students really do understand their probable career choices, it is a time for even more concentrated exploration. If the ability to test out new ideas using a career-related database is available, the guidance counselor, you, and the student can work together to explore new options. Databases in the Suggested Sources for Further Information section are excellent for information about all types of additional education and training.

After age 16, most states allow students with a work permit to be employed more hours than previously allowed. While this will vary by location from city to city and state to state, you need to help them with the process of getting a work permit. Have a poster up in a prominent place in your library that outlines the way to apply for a work permit. If you have a career counselor at school, collaborate on lunchtime workshops for work permits. Then you can help find work opportunities.

Retail, agriculture, and office work are just some of the opportunities available to high school students. While some may have to use their pay in order to add to family resources, others work to pay their car or those senior expenses such as prom or senior outings or save for college or after-graduation adventures. Providing information about the laws for working and some ideas of places where 16-year-olds may work, the types of jobs they may seek, and a little about the salaries they may command will help reduce some of their later rejection and frustration (see Chapter 5, p. 95). Create a job-search board, or even designate a conference room to display these materials, a small room where students can meet, discuss, and share those resources. It is a good place where groups of students may research and report to their colleagues about job openings and good or maybe not-so-good places to work, among other information they can share.

High school teachers, counselors, and librarians have always wondered about how to help those students who do not seem to want any help. They are skipping school because they see no reason to go to school. Classes do not seem to offer them anything they see as practical to their lives. This begins long before high school, but if there is any way to keep these students in school until they graduate, the chance that they will have a better life is definitely increased. Allowing the library to be a place where students can choose to do less academically challenging activities that keep them in school, such as providing technologies that can read their texts to them, may help them understand enough to pass tests and even begin to score higher on tests.

Encouraging any students who appear disinterested to become a part of the school by helping them to find a connection, in classes or through clubs, work, or helping you with a special project that builds upon their talents, or sometimes just being a helpful listener can make a big difference that encourages them to hang on until they finish their requirements. One author had a small room next to the library office where, over a three-year period, a small group of three students hung out before school and at lunch. They were not engaged with any school activities but could occasionally be drafted into helping with library projects like creating brochures and mending books. They continued meeting in the library up until the date of graduation, and when they left, they remarked that they did not think they could have made it through the years without the refuge and space that the library offered. Many librarians have stories like this, and one of the strengths of school librarians lies in their ability to make students like these feel welcome. Continuing to offer resources through the school, the local community college, adult school, or other agency can keep all students thinking about their options. As a school librarian, you manage a facility that is less structured than the classroom. It can become an oasis for those who need a quiet room, a space away from the noise to just relax.

Students will learn quickly if you are a person who can help answer questions, the easy ones and then the more difficult, which are those that personally affect a student's life. You need to be prepared to listen if a student needs help because of a home situation, a bully in the school, the need to change courses in the school, or any other personal need. Coming into the library to seek help does not involve waiting in those few moments at the beginning or ending of a class to talk to the teacher or making an appointment with the guidance counselor. It is often difficult to try to talk to other teachers who have students constantly coming into the room for class and leaving when the bell rings. It does not leave much time to talk privately. Waiting outside the counselor's office has its own interpretation by other students. While you may not be able to solve every problem, you might be able to relieve a little anxiety and make some positive suggestions to repair a situation. In some cases, it may involve bringing in outside help, which will mean talking the situation over with the counselor, principal, and any others who may be involved. The key is to keep the confidence of students and do everything you can to help them gain the strength and knowledge they need to solve the problems that face your students.

For the college-bound student, your work with the guidance counselor to provide software packages that allow students to take practice tests for both PSAT and SAT tests can alleviate some of the anxiety students may have for these hurdles. Working with the public librarian, this type of testing practice is made available at the public library for times when school is not in session both during the school year and over the summer vacation. Many public libraries offer test prep workshops, so keep your eye out for those kinds of programs and publicize them. You can continue to offer resources that help such as testing books for other types of tests, including tests for the military, trade school, and apprenticeships. Be sure to include career sets of books, career databases, and compelling biographies and fiction that show the many options available.

Education Environment

Students beginning in the eleventh grade need to know the choices that will face them in two short years. Not only can they learn about them but, for some, they can also begin an option while they are still in high school. Some high schools offer training that moves graduates directly into the workforce. These would include administrative skills in preparation for work in offices, giving them up-to-date knowledge of the various technologies available for composing, printing, and filing correspondence, basic bookkeeping as well as communication skills so they work well with others and can meet the public in any capacity whether on the phone or at the reception desk. For others, beauty salon and barber shop state-license preparation that would cost time and fees after graduation are available as a track within their high school coursework. Both male and female students need to be encouraged to take this track. For still others, basic car repair, construction skills, plumbing, and electrical repair will prepare students for positions in companies, small and large, allowing them to begin to work and consider additional training to increase skills as a part of that job or to make a change to a different company. Larger school districts or county districts may have a central training facility, allowing students to arrange classes for half days in their academic programs and then go for the other half-day sessions in a technical center.

If your high school or school district does not have any of these possibilities as a part of the curriculum, helping students begin one of these occupations while they are in high school can be very useful. The guidance counselor may know area agencies such as beauty or barber colleges where students could be enrolled part-time while they are attending high school. It might even be possible to arrange a shortened school day for these students. These may have a fee for the training, and you and your counselors must try to help them find jobs to earn money to pay these expenses.

Helping students find part-time jobs before they finish high school will provide funds for them for courses or for other expenses, such as class trips or social activities. Working with the guidance counselor, gather the information about what is required at what age and what can a student legally do when working in any job and what skills are required to be able to apply. Getting a work permit was discussed in Chapter 5 (p. 100) and earlier in this chapter. That information was general. When it is time to actually apply for this, where does one go to apply, what documents are needed such as birth certificate, if anyone's signature is required except the applicants, and is there a fee? Knowing the rules for an employee with a work permit will save the student the embarrassment of applying for a job the permit will not allow. Students often can work in stock rooms of department and grocery stores while they will not be old enough to serve liquor to patrons. Having that information will be helpful for all students. Money earned and saved can go a long way to paying for any training program after high school.

Another opportunity to get some practice working before graduation is to apply for an internship or accept an assignment for service learning. These are both volunteer and paid in local businesses and are becoming a requirement for some high schools. Working with the guidance counselor to create the database of these local opportunities is very helpful, and it is a database that will need constant upkeep as people and businesses change frequently. ▧ Using student assistants or volunteers to help with this would be informative for them as well as helpful for both the librarian and the guidance counselor.

For students who are interested in further education, the PSAT and SAT exams may seem the primary focus, but no matter that score, students must continue those activities and grade points needed to get into the college they want to attend. They will begin to face the writing skills to complete those required essays for the application process. These are supposedly the responsibilities of the student, but they are often reviewed by parents and others. As stated in the previous chapter, admissions requirements are constantly changing, and while the essay may be phasing out, there will no doubt be other ways that universities and colleges will test student abilities to write a clear and thoughtful essay. Working with those teachers who cover writing skills is helpful with this process. Students should not say they plan to join the Peace Corps upon college graduation if they have no interest at all in such an endeavor. However, a student who was given the opportunity to build homes in another country over one high school summer may indeed be a candidate for the Peace Corps. Reality and honesty are paramount in the carefully crafted, well-written essay.

Advanced Placement (AP) courses, while more work than other classes, can help students start college with credits already collected, thus saving tuition for a similar course. This has been discussed in the previous chapter, but if eleventh-grade students did not choose that option and wish to change their course schedules, it needs to be done as soon as possible. If they have missed this opportunity, some community colleges allow students to take classes there while they are still in high school, and other opportunities such as on-line courses offered through the school can make up for any missing opportunities along the way.

Those students who are able to join an apprenticeship program will be compensated for their work while they are learning. Most other students will need to calculate the costs of their next education. Calculating these costs includes travel to and from campus even for those who remain at home, tuition, books, any lab fees, and other expenses; for those students who go away to schools, they must add the cost of dormitory and meals. Making a realistic assessment of these factors is an important step in the decision-making process. It is also time for them to be thinking about the opportunities for funding these costs.

All students should be made aware of the opportunities for scholarships. Some small merit scholarships may be awarded locally to high school seniors and scholarships. Others may be available to students in their state institutions if they are the top students in their high school class. Other excellent universities offer scholarships for good students to increase the diversity of the students at a given university. They may be as much as tuition and housing for four years if the student maintains an adequate grade point average. Many of these potential students are from homes where no member of the family has gone to college and where the culture is one that makes it difficult for parents to allow their child to move from the safety and security of the family to travel away from home for this scholarship. Your informal discussions with these students, and perhaps their parents, can help them to see that their lives will certainly change, and it may be scary, but it will be worth the adventure.

Other students come from homes where the parents' income will make them ineligible for scholarships based on need, but their families may not be able to cover the high cost of a four-year education. In reality, they are as needy as a less financially able family, and they will need help with these costs. You and the counselor work together to identify able students and discuss the possibilities for available funding and help students make applications to appropriate sites for scholarship funding.

Students who are participating in athletic programs may be seeking scholarships for sports at a university as an excellent way to cut expenses. School coaches are very aware of the options for any star athlete who has gained attention. These young men and women are probably already on the radar with college scouts calling on them and their parents seeking their signature on a plan to attend. You can help the families understand the time commitment playing on a team with early and late practice before and after classes, missing classes for out-of-town games, and the possibility of taking fewer courses, making the potential time to degree longer. The challenge for your "star" is that when this student reaches that college team, stars from other high schools across the country will be competing, and the competition will be tough. The "carrot" that a college athlete can move to the pros is equally challenging since most colleges have only one and sometimes no student chosen at the end of the year in the pro-draft.

Other good athletes will need to have some indication of their chances for playing at an academic institution. Good players in high school will be arriving on campus with their competition against good players as well as stars from other high schools. If it is a highly ranked university with a winning team, that competition will come, not only from the United States but even from other countries. It is not a given that your good athletic will even make the team.

Working with coaches, an analysis of the school where they may be more likely to have financial assistance may be helpful. Matching this with the curriculum they will want to follow may send them back to your databases to check the quality of the academic program with the athletic opportunities. Students and their parents may see this path as without obstacles, but hurdles are there, and being on a team is not a sure thing, so for student athletes, getting an education should be the major goal. Other funding is also available. One of the book's authors has a nephew who was a star player on his university baseball team, but his scholarship was an academic scholarship that was not dependent upon his athletic success.

Students will need to determine the cost of their education at the institution they choose, and they need to calculate the actual cost of borrowing money to attend that school when starting at a community college closer to home for two years may be a better financial choice. Calculating this will be discussed under Economic Awareness.

With the education and training options considered, it is time to match those options to what to do after graduation. This depends on the career that students wish to pursue.

Career Information

Career counseling begins in earnest during these two years. Students will need to make that final decision whether to go immediately to work or to pursue training or further education. As much as one would hope that every student had the desire to continue formal learning after high school, this may not be possible. Nevertheless, they may need even more information about the opportunities for them in the workplace. Identifying persons who have interesting jobs and can talk about why they decided on that job and how they went about becoming employed will be helpful. Providing students with opportunities to learn about the wide variety of careers that are open to them, including part-time work, will allow your students to continue exploring, continue learning, and have their questions answered about the workplace, the salary, the benefits, the locations, and uniforms or dress codes. These are all things most young people think they know but often have no concrete evidence to support that knowledge. If it is possible, organizing a career fair for students who are not interested in college could give some firsthand information about jobs and also about internships and apprenticeships.

The opportunity of the military may appeal to a high school graduate for a variety of reasons, from wishing to serve his or her country to wanting to obtain further education through military service. While the military does offer this, students and their parents need to understand that the military recruiter is a salesperson. Making sure to do their due diligence by following up with research and discussion within all the branches of the military can assure students and their families that they are making a more informed decision. Remind students of the Question Formulation Technique (QFT) and how they can brainstorm all the questions they have before visiting with the recruiter. Be sure to take the questions with them to the interview and make sure they are all answered. Questions include grades, ability to serve if they have had police trouble, the possibilities of obtaining a college degree, years of service required to be eligible for college courses, where they might be sent for their service, and if there is any guarantee of pursuing a particular vocational path through military service. Asking a recruiter to come to the school to discuss the military and requirements for finishing high school or the GED can be helpful.

A student who is interested in a military career can consider Reserve Officers' Training Corps (ROTC) if it is offered in your school program and the possibility of ROTC in the college they are planning to attend because this offers tuition assistance. Your students should also find out exactly by whom and how appointments are made to the military academies. A four-year degree and an appointment as an officer await upon graduation to those who are admitted to and graduate from West Point, Annapolis, or the Air Force Academy in Colorado Springs. Again, the competition is great, but the opportunity is there.

The goal is to provide as much information as possible about actual careers that need research. In one of the authors' school, the librarian and the career counselor created a career library of materials, including college catalogs, career books, test prep books, and other print and online resources that resided in the career center but were checked out through the library. The library hosted the career database for all to use. Collaborating to invite speakers, hold job seminars, and hold work permit meetings made the library and career center active sites for students to get information they need. If your school does not have such a position, creating a "career corner" with similar materials, collaborating with counselors to invite speakers in, and holding job fairs and other events can make college and career preparation a bit easier. College information recruiters, military recruiters, and others can stop by to chat with students in the career center room or your career corner.

Some high schools have career counselors on staff who can help students and their families fill out college forms, find internships, and help students make college decisions. If your school is lucky enough to have such a position, a librarian and career counselor collaboration is a perfect way to bring resources to students and provide a forum to help them. Many have already made their decisions, but if not, consider hosting a university fair in your school, district, or county where the colleges can send representatives to talk with students about what they offer. What is very important here is to get as many students as possible to be interested, even those for whom the expenses for any education after high school make it seem impossible. For this group of students, it is important to get parents to the school. You and your counselors need to find out if parents or other family members do not see higher education as necessary in the lives of their children, or they may be, for cultural reasons, fearful of their children going out to attend a school away from the home. Sharing how their capable child can achieve a college education may pave the way for other siblings in the home.

Electronic simulations and other programs offer students some ways to test their abilities for higher education. Placing information where they are located and an open desk for a student to either use the computer there or access a personal laptop make this easily accessible. A poster attracting students to that website with instructions for how to use it, all developed by one or more service learning students, will add to your resources at little effort from you.

Many opportunities are available for funding that is not borrowing money. Some of these suggestions are discussed in the following paragraphs. How to help students with the financial obligation of college is discussed in the next section.

As stated earlier, one of the most appealing routes for students who are good athletes is the college sports scholarship that may include full tuition, housing, and meals until they graduate. If the candidate is excellent in the sport but less a student, tutoring is often a part of this process. To maintain a scholarship, the student must be able to participate in the season's games, and that means maintaining an adequate grade point average. For many students, the time required for practice and going to away games makes it difficult to carry more than the minimum number of courses, which may extend the time to graduate beyond four years. Also, if an athlete cannot maintain those grades, this person can be dropped from the team. The other challenge in this route is the chance for injury leaving a player off the roster and, if really serious, out of the game for the duration, which means loss of scholarship. Another challenge comes from alumni from the university and their eagerness to "help out" with expenses. The National Collegiate Athletic Association (NCAA) has very strict rules for what benefits can be offered to potential students and athletes after they arrive on campus. One author served on a university Senate Athletic Committee, and this may even seem ridiculous, but she could not buy her high-school-football-playing nephew a sweatshirt with the school logo on it because it could be construed as interfering with the recruitment process. Alums often want to help a student whose parents have little ability to help him or her get home for the holidays, but buying that ticket is not legal and could cost the university its eligibility.

These are all factors that will be difficult for a high school athlete to assimilate and perhaps even more difficult for parents who have stars in their eyes. However, sometimes a high school football player who was a star athlete and has this opportunity can succeed where it is highly likely that this student would become a gang member and that young man's life could have had a very different outcome.

Students who come from homes where there seems to be less opportunity to go to one of those most sought-after and also most expensive programs may find that, if their grades and SAT scores are high, they may receive scholarships and grants that will allow them to attend those programs at no cost to their parents. These are usually to those schools with huge endowments for scholarships, and they do place students in dormitories and classroom with others who will go to Switzerland skiing on holidays when they may not even be able to afford a trip home for a holiday. These able students have many opportunities if they are eligible for admission. Universities that are trying to raise the number of applicants representing a diverse student body may not only bring students to campus before other freshmen for an orientation but also provide students a clothing allowance in case they need a more college-oriented wardrobe. These opportunities give them a way to ease into their new environment and also pave the way upon graduation for interested alumni to help them enter the workplace. Students who have accepted their college's invitation to enroll are almost immediately asked to make decisions about courses for their first semester. This comes when they are uncertain about their career plans. Others may have some idea but need a realistic assessment.

Some students have made a conscious choice of their career path by their senior year; they have a goal in mind, but that may just as easily change after they begin college. The lead in the high school musical may find that the competition in a vocal music program may not lead to a role in a Broadway musical; how many students heading for that medical degree find they are less interested after their college chemistry class? You can provide the information they will need to follow for an alternate choice that would be equally interesting. These students are ready to learn what each career choice and potential alternate choice means in the workplace.

The five-year-old who chose to be an airline pilot and has steadfastly kept that goal needs to meet an actual airline pilot to help confirm and understand the reality of the time, effort, and expense for hours in the air to get those flying credentials, followed by the years on the job to move from a very junior position in a smaller plane for an airline to commanding an airbus. At least that student will have a better idea of the financial commitment to the goal and will make sure it is the best career choice with an alternate related to a different career, but still with an airline.

As discussed in Chapter 2, biographies are good places to begin research on career paths. They may be especially helpful about those people working in the seemingly more glamorous professions; learning of their challenges as well as their successes begins the discussion of what role fame and fortune play in their lives along with the high salaries. Reading newspaper articles can trace the lives of sports heroes and government officials, some of whom have withstood the pressure fame has placed on them and others who have not fared as well in the media.

Students may begin to assess their competencies related to the role in the career of their choice, whether they have the personality to sell products, the capability to wait for that promotion in a highly competitive workplace, or the aggressiveness needed to go for yet another audition after failing several. Adding these factors to the cost of preparing for that career may help them start their training or university with a more open mind to the path ahead.

You and your guidance counselor have helped students find training and further education opportunities while providing a more realistic analysis of the careers they have chosen. Now they must match those choices and alternate choices with the actual cost of pursuing these opportunities and also address the expenses that come with being a junior or senior in high school.

Economic Awareness

Previously, students have been asked to consider the economics of their lives in terms of the immediate. At this time their consideration of the present continues, while they turn their focus on the future. For the present, those students who are deciding whether or not to go for their driving test need to conduct a little research that can help them understand the increased cost of insurance on the family automobile for a teenage driver. If they are going to work immediately after high school and will need a car, they should learn the costs associated with owning that car and paying for the insurance. That involves the yearly license fee and the cost of gasoline, tires, and other maintenance.

While students have most likely been going out in groups since junior high, these years of high school are when couples seem to form and they begin to go out on dates. Dating behavior and expectations for who pays include sharing costs, meeting at the venue, or just hanging out in a local park or at home; they vary not just by state or city but also by school. Financial considerations come up for teens regardless of the school culture and will be a large part of the teen life in high school. School dances may be important to some, with the expenses of homecoming and ultimately prom impacting student and family budgets. Library workshops or events can include fun activities and allow discussion about present-day expectations for social events.

This is an excellent time for students to have accurate information on managing finances, including an introduction to a pay stub with deductions such as internal revenue and state taxes, social security, and health insurance. While not all these may be deducted at this time from a part-time salary, taxes may be. When they are "self-employed" as babysitters or mowing lawns, nothing will be automatically taken out of those earnings. Their parents may be interested if those earnings reach a level that the student is no longer considered their dependent. A longer activity allows students to take a "Bite of Reality."

> Joanne T. Crotts, librarian in the Skinner Library, Asheville School, Asheville, North Carolina, reports that they bring in representatives from a local bank who talk to seniors about saving money, the allure and pitfalls of credit cards, and how to establish credit among other money matters.

Providing exercises for students to help them understand other costs is covered in Chapter 7. However, introductions to household budgets can go along with finding out the cost of insurance for underage students driving a family vehicle.

> Leslie Poston and her teachers at the Kiski School in Saltsburg, Pennsylvania, have a collaborative unit on Personal Finance and Independent Living. In this all-boys school, students are grouped in families who maintain a household budget with scenarios that require making choices on expenditures.

While students who are going to work immediately after high school will need to plan for those expenses, this process is covered in Chapter 7. Here, those students who are considering higher education need to determine the cost of one year at any school(s) where they would like to attend. This has been discussed in previous chapters, but it is immediately on the horizon here. Costs, especially tuition, may have changed even since the last year. One solution many students choose is to attend their local community college for their first two years, completing their general education requirements at a lesser expense. Attending school and working to save for the last two years at a university or college can certainly reduce the amount of debt that needs repaying after college.

Student loans are a major method of paying for college, but there are many pros and cons to doing so. Graduating with a six-figure debt makes it difficult to see how this can be paid back on a beginning salary; these debts begin to be collected upon graduation, and they do not go away. Inviting someone to come from a local bank to talk about borrowing money for college will provide some information and allow students to ask any questions they might have. Another person who would be helpful is someone from a training program, a community college, or a local college who can explain those funds available to attend that institution.

Civic Responsibility

In our democratic society, ordinary citizens are given a great many freedoms. One might argue that the greatest is dissent. Citizens have the right to criticize the government, and along with this freedom come the ability and responsibility to participate. Students are taught this in their classes, and they read the U.S. Constitution and the Bill of Rights and study the historical context for their creation. Frank Zappa questions whether students are being taught when he said in an interview,

> One of the things that was taken out of the curriculum was civics. Civics was a class that used to be required before you could graduate from high school. You were taught what was in the U.S. Constitution. And after all the student rebellions in the '60s, civics was banished from the student curriculum and was replaced by something called social studies. Here we live in a country that has a fabulous constitution and all these guarantees, a contract between the citizens and the government—nobody knows what's in it. It's one of the best kept secrets. And so, if you don't know what your rights are, how can you stand up for them? And furthermore, if you don't know what is in that document, how can you care if someone is shredding it?[1]

You can check with your teachers to confirm or deny Zappa's analysis, and depending upon their response, you may need to help students understand that citizens must obey laws and pay taxes, they must register for the draft, and they are obligated to be witnesses and members of juries. Citizens are not required to vote in the United States, but it is a right and an honor to be able to do so. Being able to vote can be practiced in high school with the various elections there.

Elections in high school can include class presidents, student-council officers and members, presidents of the various clubs in the school, and team captains of the athletic teams. All these start the process of participating in voting and prepare them for an election for a local, state, or national election. Encouraging students to make posters and signs with clever slogans is excellent training for adult clubs and supporting a candidate for an election and can even predict their becoming a candidate themselves. Some school districts have high school students elected to the school board, which drives home the role of the school board, and how and what happens at a school board meeting impacts the students in the school. Some towns have teen advisory boards to their councils in which interested students can join, while community clubs, nonprofit organizations, and libraries may offer teen advisory roles.

Seniors in high school are reaching the age when they can register to vote so that government by the people and for the people is quickly going to become their duty to help choose their government, accepting the responsibility of being a citizen. They need to learn how to assess candidates, what they promise, and what they have done in the past so that as new voters, they can be intelligent voters. Recognition that they need to vote and that their vote truly does count is an important aspect of civic responsibility that all students should come away with as they leave school.

Students are most likely to identify with the political party of their parents, and they will hear a great deal about the candidates when they are discussed in their homes. This identification may or may not last, as students begin to research on their own, or as they review their decisions as young adults. One of your jobs is to ensure that they know how to identify the source of their political information and be able to evaluate that source for perspective and possible bias. It is good for students to see parents who vote in an election and that they have modeled the behavior of participating in their rights and responsibilities. For avid members of any party, it is sometimes difficult to see virtues of any other candidate who is not a member of that party, but continued modeling of polite civic discourse is important. You can hold debates, and you can, if you are inclined, help to lead a debate club or any other club that helps model the many roles of good citizenship.

One way for students to get to know candidates for office is to volunteer with their campaigns. High school students are welcome volunteers, and it is an opportunity to get to know the members of city and county council and the mayor or county commissioner. They can distribute flyers, help with mailings to constituents, and perhaps even help with telephone calls to find out just which candidate voters might be going to support and to encourage them to go to the polls. This helps students improve their communication skills as well as learning the political process. If students are working with a candidate, try to provide them with a forum to share what they are doing and how this office is working to help with the election. Students can move from these efforts into the wider world of Congress.

The greater learning experience is that these people are human beings who serve their constituents. They will be responding to complaints and demonstrating the steps necessary to make improvements. Students can also see the many protocols used when meeting with an official and how to make a case to solve a problem. Going to see an official does require some planning if the time in the office is to be productive.

While an opportunity to go to Washington, DC, and work in a congressional office as a junior or senior in high school is not readily available, a student who has been active in working on a political campaign may find that such an opportunity may open up for him or her. Students working in any political arena discover that networking is an important part of making things happen and can walk away from such an experience with the confidence that they can meet people and converse with much more ease than when they first began. Going to Washington is not the only way to meet a member of Congress.

Meeting a legislator can also be someone from state government as well as a member of Congress. This can also be enhanced with an opportunity to meet a local legislator in the school. It may be easier to have this happen at this level since this guest will be talking to potential voters in the next election.

Many high school seniors will be eligible to vote in the next election if they have registered to vote. As introduced in Chapter 5, Activity 15 (p. 89), Tamara Cox at Wren High School in Piedmont, South Carolina, has an excellent way to encourage voting:

> When it is time for students to vote for our state book award, I invite our county's voting commission to our school. They bring voting booths and voter's registration forms so that students can vote for their favorite book on a real voting machine and register to vote (if they're old enough). I also set up a display with pictures and short bios of our local, state, and federal government officials as well as a link to a quiz that helps them determine which political party fits the best with their opinions. In times of political controversy, such as the March for Our Lives and net neutrality vote, I put out paper, pens, and the addresses of our elected officials.
>
> Finally, when I'm collecting library materials and Chromebooks, I put up a display with voter's registration forms so that they have one more chance to grab a form and register before graduation.

Social media has become such an important part of all of our lives and those of our students. How this affects the process of being a citizen is something to be investigated within their courses. If possible, work with your civics, history, government, or English teachers to help students understand the process of social media in the world today. The use of social media and the effect on elections remain a hot topic. Any of your students who are working or have worked with candidates in elections could bring together what they think worked best and what needed improvement and then see during the next election what changes were made. They might even make some suggestions for different ways to carry out the process.

Two civic responsibilities of everyone in the school include working together and diligently to keep students aware of the problems of incorrectly using social media and of allowing bullying to happen; sometimes these are interrelated. It may be an urban legend that college admission officers troll social media to help make decisions between two equally qualified candidates for entrance in their school, but who wants to test this? What you say about or show to anyone can go viral with the click of that cell phone. A student may never know that it was that click of that one message that denied him or her entrance in the school of his or her choice. And the student may never know that what he or she said about a fellow student affected that person's life in a disastrous way. Encourage students to understand that social media can effect positive change; showing off the work that they do in a positive way that works for them lets others see this online. These positives can go far in helping other students see the positive benefits of posting well.

Students need to be reminded often of their civic responsibility to help others, and this may mean trying to detour the outcome of poorly thought out and inappropriate uses of social media and to minimize the effects of bullying in person or on social media. To support a student who is being bullied may turn the wrath of those doing the bullying onto the potential "knight in shining armor." Reporting bullying is not ratting out a friend or comrade; rather it is being responsible in a civil society. Again, the library is that quiet place where students can report themselves or someone else being bullied, and you can take the appropriate action moving that first step away from the student and onto the proper teacher, administrator, or even the police. Make sure to check in with health and physical education teachers to see if you can drop in to give lessons on the impacts of bullying, including physical, verbal, social, relational, and cyber, and how students can become responsible allies for their friends.

Civic responsibility also means learning and obeying local, state, and national laws established by the officials governing citizens. Students are made aware of the school's rules governing them that are explained when they enter the high school. Penalties for misbehavior may have many outcomes, including being suspended for a number of days. Such a record will affect getting a job or being admitted to a school. Students who are taking driver's education will be made aware of the rules of the road, but other rules may not be as often even discussed. The seniors are approaching that eighteenth birthday, and that date moves them into a different category. Finding speakers to present programs for these students may help them understand the outcomes of what may have been considered a prank.

Joanne T. Crotts, Asheville School, brings in a local lawyer who talks to the seniors about what that age means legally now and what they can be held accountable for doing.

Civic engagement includes helping community members, and high school is the perfect time to participate in their community by volunteering or joining others when needed during disasters or other times of need. Helping to put on local events like farmer's markets, parades, art shows, music festivals, or other events on the basis of student interests helps to create community goodwill. Working to get citizens to register to vote and even to help them get to the polls on Election Day are two ways to volunteer even before your students are eligible to vote. All these volunteer efforts create that important network of adults and peers who can help them gain the confidence they can use the rest of their lives, and any one of these adults may be able to support them some way.

Most high school students take courses in government and economics. In these classes, students learn not only how the government works but also why it works that way, what other forms of governments there are, and why and how they can work to create policies that move their communities forward. You can encourage students to research effectively those topics of interest and importance to them and help them to make their decisions on the basis of solid evidence and positive forward movement. Finding that solid evidence requires careful research.

These two years are your last chance to make sure your students know how to read, listen, and view information so they can confirm its accuracy, recognize its bias, and check a variety of sources for clarity. It is a time for students to do deep research into news on social media, in print, on television, or any other source. This means they will have what they need to work to effect change.

Those who feel a connection to making change have all the opportunities listed earlier: working for candidates, volunteering, and participating on teen advisory boards to help the adults in their world understand their perspective and honor it as another voice in the democratic process. Having their voices heard can mean writing letters to the editor of the local newspaper or the people who are responsible for what they are supporting. That persuasive letter discussed in Chapter 3 is even more important here.

While the concentration in this chapter has been on getting students ready to take that next step into becoming adults, it has not really addressed the wide world that they face once they leave the structure and safety of their K–12 education. The responsibilities and the activities discussed in the previous chapters have gone beyond your more structured assignment to collaborate with teachers and ensure information skills. These chapters have challenged you to take a leadership role in making sure students leave high school knowing what they must do to succeed. However, before students move on and walk out our doors, they still have some advice you may want to give to your students. Chapter 7 will address some of these possibilities.

Suggested Activities

Responsibilities for the Librarian

1. Time management has many facets. Brenda Hough in her book for librarians, *Time Management for Library Staff* (Santa Barbara, CA: Libraries Unlimited, 2018), has a simple chart for students to prioritize their lives. They can also create a similar chart that would let them place their assignments with a prioritization but giving them the opportunity to put the deadline and make an estimate of what they need to do and the time each step would take.

Goals	Personal or Work Life	Short Term or Long Term	High, Medium, or Low Priority

Another way to track time is to combine the schedules of assignments due from every class, and appointments, meetings, practices, work, and any other commitments are greatly eased by a calendar on laptop, notebook, or cell phone. You or one of your geek squad can offer this service during a brown-bag lunch or with an appointment before or after school. If any of your teachers still need this information, you can expand your audience adding them.

Education Environment

2. Providing students at this level with the possibility of both paid and volunteer internships will help them "test" an occupation and places to go for service learning. These open the door to watching how those involved "practice" their profession, and seeing the workplace from inside may help students rethink their career choice. Keeping the list of internships up to date should be assigned to a student volunteer or community-service student to relieve you of this responsibility. It will be very helpful to any student with this interest.

Does your school maintain an electronic list of service opportunities for students to use when they are assigned that service requirement? If yes, check it out. Even if one exists and especially if no such list is available, ask teachers, students, parents, and members of the community to help you create a list of places where students can gain experience either by volunteering or with some payment for their services. Maintaining this electronic list should be an assignment of one or more of your students.

Career Information

3. Plan a Career Technical Education (CTE) maker fair for students who are not planning to attend college. If your school has vocational courses, invite students to come

into the library and help other students to create an object from their classroom: metal class, sewing, cooking class, and auto class. Ask them to demonstrate how to change the oil in your car or design a chair. See if you can get the CTE classes to join with an English and art class to write up directions for changing that oil in the car and then create an infographic to share with the school.

4. If no technical training is available in your school, invite members of the community to discuss their training, their workplace, a salary range, and how to join that profession. With the guidance counselor, gather information about training possibilities such as beauty and barber colleges, technical training schools, and apprenticeships.

5. Encourage cross-class networking so that the AP students planning to become architects meet with the woodworking students to create something. Demonstrate that the arts, sciences, and vocational worlds are intertwined.

6. CTE students may never set foot in a school once they leave high school. Apprenticeships and other on-the-job training give them the skills they need. While you still have them in high school, consider collaborating with their teachers to provide some hands-on civics activities to encourage them to consider themselves to be community leaders. Invite union officials to come talk to the class, business people who belong to community organizations that provide scholarships, and entrepreneurs who have created businesses with the skills they learned in their CTE classes.

7. Have students look up the U.S. military academy of interest to them. They will then need to review the requirements, such as SAT scores for admission and the process for nomination, and then see if they meet the minimum requirements. Who would be involved in the nomination process, and how would they contact that person? A student interested in a career as an officer in the military might also want to see about ROTC in the university where they are planning to attend.

8. Organizing a college forum may not be necessary if you are living in a large city, and this type of opportunity is provided for all students in the area. Then you only need to encourage students and their parents to attend. If you are in a much smaller city or rural area, you should try to do this for your students, especially if not many of them plan to go to college. You have three additional ways to do this. The first is to find the recruitment team at the nearest colleges and community colleges. If they are able to attend such a forum, then principal and guidance counselor select a date and invite these persons to come to talk to students and their parents. If this is not possible, the second opportunity is to ask your teachers. This may not be too helpful if they all attended schools in other states, but if they are willing to help, you can send letters to the colleges and universities that your teachers attended and ask them to send information about enrolling in their institution. At your forum, your teachers can share this information, encouraging students to apply for admission. A third might be to enlist the help of parents who are alumni of nearby community colleges and universities.

Finally, college admission offices from small colleges around the country will often make recruiting trips; contact them and get your high school on their radar. Advertise this possibility as soon as you have the date, and when they arrive, you can announce their visit in the morning for a lunchtime interview.

9. Another opportunity to share with students is Career Cruising: https://public .careercruising.com/en/. This package covers career options, interest assessments, and games, as well as planning for college and financial literacy.

   Roseanne Cipolone also suggests using the SAT Question of the day as a way to continue studying with daily, quick practice (http://media.collegeboard.com/email/ libraries/samples/sample_qotd.html) Your public library may also have SAT and ACT workshops in conjunction with local universities and colleges.

Economic Awareness

10. Many careers are available for students who have no desire to go to an academic institution. Have luncheon meetings to meet persons from local shops and corporations who can share what they do and how they learned how to do it. Students can see the roles of these persons in the community, and they can answer questions and make suggestions for those who are interested in this working environment.

11. Pay stubs usually show the amount of earning with deductions for local, state, and national income taxes, social security or other retirement plan, and health insurance. If the employee has other deductions such as union dues, or charges for parking spaces at the location, those will also appear there. If you can find examples of actual pay stubs that will not identify the owner, these will be helpful. Otherwise you can create a handout with this information.

12. A learning opportunity for seniors is as close as your nearest Credit Union. In California and Nevada, the program is called "Bite of Reality." According to Tena Lozano, the executive director of the Richard Myles Johnson (RMJ) Foundation, who sponsors "Bite of Reality," other states have similar programs under different names, often called "Reality Fairs.[2] Check your nearest Credit Union to see if they offer this program: http://www.rmjfoundation.org/index.php/bite-of-reality (https://www .ncuf.coop/how-we-help/fairs-simulations/reality-fairs/reality-fairs.cmsx).

   The following text is quoted from the RMJ Foundation site, http://www .rmjfoundation.org/index.php/bite-of-reality:

   > Bite of Reality is a hands-on app based simulation that appeals to teens while giving them a taste of real-world financial realities. Teens are given a fictional occupation, salary, spouse and family, student loan debt, credit card debt, and medical insurance payments. The teens then walk around to various table-top stations to "purchase" housing, transportation, food, clothing, household necessities, day care, and

other needs. Fortunately, the game also includes a "credit union" to help with their financial needs.

You can rearrange all furniture to create the "stations" where students would come by to "purchase" items. Cards were placed with different products on them with accompanying prices. Those of us volunteers sitting behind the desk played the roles of shopkeeper and tried to "sell" the most expensive products possible. Students were given a brief introduction and then let loose to decide what items they needed in order to have the best life possible.

13. What will be interesting from an adult perspective is to talk with the participants about their purchases and how to decide what was "needed" and what was "wanted." For example, those who choose to have families to support along with repaying student loans and car payments will find out pretty quickly that the kind of car they chose would determine how high the payments would be and how that would impact their income.

14. Calculating the costs of attending any training or higher education institution was begun in grades 9–10. Review Activity 10 in Chapter 5 and have students update this electronic resource. For the school(s) of their choice, have students research all costs of attending, reminding them of the need to travel to and from school for holidays. These expenses need to be put into the tabulation as well as tuition, housing, books, and any related expenses, such as tickets to athletic events, and perhaps whether or not they want to pledge a sorority or fraternity.

15. Invite someone from a nearby college to discuss both the opportunities for scholarship availability and the agencies that might lend funds to students to cover their tuition. Some states allow students to borrow money and then allow them to pay it back by becoming a teacher within the state. Other funds are available from the federal government, but borrowing here needs to be explained very carefully because these funds become available for repayment upon graduation or leaving school before graduation.

16. If at all possible, you might invite someone from a bank to come in and talk about borrowing the money that will be needed to attend the university for all four years if the tuition, books, and other expenses all remain the same. If they have done any research on the probable income of any position in which they have an interest, this may help them see the percentage that such a debt will take from their salary.

Civic Responsibility

17. The meaning of voting in a democratic society is critical for young people today. They need to be shown how to register to vote, where voting is held, using mailed-in voting opportunities, and reading the documentation that comes to homes where registered voters live. This will be in posted flyers from candidates, information from the League of Women Voters, among others. Perhaps a member of the League of Women Voters

could come to your school in the months before a national or state election to explain this process. On election days, you should go to vote before school opens so you can display your "I voted" sticker you are given after voting. Offer small incentives such as a cup of cocoa or lemonade in the library to those students old enough to vote to come to the library wearing their "I voted" sticker.

18. When a group of students has a critical need to discuss an issue or concern with an elected official, they should research how to make an appointment with this official. Decide the path to follow and identify alternatives if that first method does not work. Or, if it does not, who would be someone who would be able to respond? Would meeting with an aid be acceptable?

   To meet with elected officials and members of Congress, you can make use of the following websites:

   https://www.aclu.org/meeting-your-elected-representatives

   https://www.usa.gov/elected-officials

   https://www.aska.org/Advocacy/grassroots/Visiting-Your-Local-Congressional-Office/

   www.ncte.org/action/reqappt

   https://www.npr.org/2014/03/26/294361018/how-to-meet-your-congressman

   Another possibility is to check out iCivics.org. Close to an election night in your town, invite a local legislator to attend an evening of government discovery. Work together to understand how the three branches of the legislature need to work in order to provide checks, balances, and collaboration. Be sure to offer food and end with handing out voter registration or go online and help students sign on.

   Learn together and see how many problems can be solved through collaboration, discussion, and open minds (https://www.icivics.org/democracyatplay-family). If an evening event does not work, try offering one at lunch. Bring in pizza and help students work together and be sure to have discussions before the final lunch. If your government or history teacher is willing, see if students can get class credit for attending.

19. Determine the agenda for the meeting. Who would speak for the group? What would be the major points to present? What would be the next sentence or the point if you do not have an adequate response?

Suggested Resources for Further Information

Williams, Connie. "From School to Community: Inspiring Student Activism." *School Library Connection*. May/June 2018, 28.

Williams, Connie. *Got Civics? Knowledge Quest* (blog). June 2018. https://knowledgequest
.aasl.org/author/cwilliams/.

Subscription Resources

1. EBSCO: https://www.ebsco.com/products/research-databases/vocational-career
-collection.
2. LearningExpress Library (EBSCO).
3. ProQuest: https://www.proquest.com/products-services/pq_career_tech_ed.html.
4. Gale's Career Transitions: http://galeapps.galegroup.com/apps/auth?cause=http%3A
%2F%2Fcareertransitions.galegroup.com%2Fhome.do%3FauthCount%3D1.
5. Career Cruising: https://public.careercruising.com/en/.
6. Rosen Digital: Financial Literacy (see grades 9–10).

Web Resources

1. EducationPlanner.org.
2. Careerzone.ny.gov or https://www.cacareerzone.org/.

Notes

1. Bob Guccione Jr. "Signs of the Times," *Spin Magazine 7* (July 1991): 60.
2. E-mail correspondence. June 13, 2018.

Chapter 7

The Real World: What to Expect after Graduation

As students walk through the doors of school for the very last time, they have completed the full journey of their K–12 education. The world these young adults enter can be a very big, mostly unknown and uncharted space that may seem even larger and more threatening unless they have been prepared from that first moment they entered those doors many years before. Far too often schools, parents, and especially the students themselves focus on the today and only a little on the tomorrow. Parents, caught up in their children's activities, help them get to practices and performances, social events, and other distractions. Teachers are focused on making sure their students complete their classes and can graduate. Time is focused on that one goal: successfully finishing high school. The information in this chapter has been both introduced and expanded throughout the previous chapters. It is repeated here almost as a pseudochecklist so you can check in with your students to make sure that they have the information they need before that last day and graduation.

At each grade level from beginning to the senior year, school librarians work with their colleagues to help students carve their paths to graduation. You may represent the culmination of all those efforts to get students to graduation, and it is hoped that you can touch base with any students leaving school before they graduate. For these students, the big world faces them at a younger age with less preparation and a much greater prognosis for failure. Perhaps as they return their library or text-books, perhaps as they ask for a signature on the form for nonreturning students or per-haps with a quick stop in the hall if possible, you can give a smile and a reminder that you and your library will remain open for them should they want to come back for more information that may be of help. The public library will have job-seeking information, and there are counselors at the local college who would have information about more education. For those graduating, different opportunities are opening. However, for both the dropouts and the graduates, becoming an adult starts immediately when they walk away from school.

Choices must be made between living at home and living away from home. Accepting a position may mean finding affordable housing or finding someone to share expenses. For those new adults moving into apartments or sharing houses, there are many questions: What if sharing an apartment is a total disaster? What about the rental agreement or the need for a car loan to have transportation to go to work? For the graduate who is trying to become totally independent, how does one find a job that pays enough to cover expenses, with a little left over to go to a movie or start a savings account? How does one get a check-ing and savings account?

For those going on to college away from home, only three or four months separate them from the many questions facing them, and they also may be living with a roommate. How will this new adult learn how to get along with the roommate assigned to him or her in a college dormitory? They need to know "Where do I go if this shared living arrangement is a disaster?" Or what does this college student do if he or she has concerns? What about sharing space with someone the student does not even know?

This book is built on the premise that librarians will take a leadership role to ensure stu-dents understand what they will face when they leave high school. It is definitely an easier task if others join in the process all along the way. Certainly, your more traditional roles are in place: collaborating with teachers, making sure students are information literate, pro-viding adequate resources, and overseeing a program and a facility that allow students to learn. However, you also have opportunities to provide learning activities that students can use to practice decision making on the basis of finding resources to explore the short- and long-term consequences of those decisions.

Expectations are that some information has been covered; you will have no guarantee that previous librarians, teachers, or guidance counselors have given and reinforced this preparation for real life and becoming lifelong learners. Creating flexible, lifelong learners is more important than ever. Students today do need to recognize that the skills they learn will most likely be used across many types of jobs throughout their lives. Being able to step up and learn new skills when needed, take leadership roles, or provide teamwork as jobs change or move will help them navigate the changing needs of those hiring today and in the future. Recognizing which competencies are adequate in another position may reduce the need for additional training. How will they go about choosing an entirely different career path if their job appears to have disappeared totally?

Being financially literate is a must. These new adults have so much to contend with: credit cards, automatic payments, home/car loans, apartment leases, and more. Their ability to understand the relationship between paycheck and well-being hopefully was started by you and your teachers through lessons articulated through the grades. You need to help them be as well prepared in financial literacy as they are with information literacy.

Equally important is the recognitions that each citizen in a democracy is a part of a community and everyone has a responsibility to participate in the democratic process. Your students' civics, history, and government teachers have explained the Constitution, the three branches of government, how a law is made, and how state governments work. They may not realize that while the attention is often focused on electing governing officials, they will also be voting on bond issues to repair schools or highways or on an issue that may repeal a law that was just passed. They will vote for judges for courts, and in some areas, they may even be voting for the school board members who govern their very high school. While earning and managing enough money to be comfortable is essential, who governs the people makes the rules and laws that can help or hinder that good life.

Thankfully, not all your students will need to learn everything from school alone. Many students have parents who have covered some of the information too, or their life experiences include having to make decisions that take them into the adult world earlier than expected. As you look through this checklist of what students should know by the time they graduate, this might be the time to assess student preparedness for those things not always covered in the classroom.

Students who need help for items on the checklist that are missing from their experiences should feel comfortable to ask you for help. Your immediate attention is given to any student who trusts you enough to come to you with a problem; your listening and trying to help locate the information or persons needed to solve the problem becomes a priority. Normally, helping your students research the various components for making a decision as well as to understand the complexities of their decisions and the effects and consequences of any choice is ongoing. But with this student, and this concern, efforts are directed to specifically helping as much as you can by guiding them to the resources, people, or material that can help them solve their dilemma.

Some students may, for many reasons, be unable to decide their next step in their lives. They may not have been chosen for the school they wished to attend, or they may decide they really are not interested in working in a business that originally interested them. If this is true, and they have the resources, perhaps you could help them work with their parents so they take a gap year.

The Gap Year

Many students are totally undecided about what careers they are going to choose or the path to take to be prepared. A year away, a gap year, may be a solution. Gap-year students may be just waiting to go to college or take a job for a year while they explore new places. Many gap-year programs are available to help families decide on a plan that fits their graduate's interests. These programs can cover the type of gap year your student might like, whether it includes travel, formal or informal coursework, volunteering, internships, or learning a new language. You and the counselor or career counselor can find some of these to share with students and parents.

Education and Career Consequences Decision

While requirements for knowledge and skills to stay viable in the workforce have been covered earlier, here the attention is focused on the student who has made the decision to leave school. This is such a critical crossroad in any student's life that it is discussed again here.

School Leavers

Throughout this book, much focus was on the student who leaves high school without the diploma. This student has far fewer opportunities to succeed throughout life. If this is not addressed at all levels in school, then these young adults continue blindly to face obstacles that keep them from moving forward. The end of that path may be in a prison, and this is a costly mistake for everyone. While it may seem impossible to encourage a discouraged teen to consider taking an equivalency test, consider ways to give it a try. Tag teaming with counselors might be a solution that could help to push these students into practicing for the test during school hours and then helping them locate test dates and locations.

You and the guidance counselor can see that these students are offered test examples for success in taking this high school equivalency test, which is equally as important as preparing for the PSAT and the SAT. If those tests are administered within the school district, dates and places are pointed out. If they are not school administered, students can be given the addresses of locations, often in the public library, where the General Equivalency Diploma (GED) tests are conducted and the dates and times for the tests are given. Those students who are not old enough to take the test are encouraged to do the sample tests and visit the site where it will be administered when they are eligible.

Identifying students who are marking time until they can leave school is not always easy to determine. If they are not doing well in classes and are missing a great many days of school, they are likely in that category, and once identified, you can give them an opportunity to come to the library for one-on-one help to make the transition. Set up a job-seeking corner in the library with information about how to look for employment that will be available to them. Open job listings that you or the guidance counselor might know about are posted here, with emphasis on jobs that do not require a high school diploma. They will need to understand how to read ads for jobs and prepare for a job interview. The following job interview checklist helps them prepare for an interview. It might point out their insufficient competencies, and that might encourage them to remain in school.

Job Interview Checklist

- Read job description carefully.
- Match your competencies to each requirement.
- Note how to make an application: phone, letter, request application form.
- Complete application process: letter, form, resume.
  - *Note:* Prepare a resume for this job description, not a previous job description.
- Send or take application to appropriate address before the deadline.
- Prepare for the interview.
- Decide appropriate attire for this interview.
- Determine what you might need to take with you, such as examples of work and your high school transcript, and gather these in a folder or briefcase.
- Plan travel time to the interview so you will be on time.
- Send a thank-you note to the person who arranged the interview.

Your job-seeking information corner will include suggestions for resume writing, with some samples students have created for this corner. Their resume will be their first introduction to prospective employers. Roseanne Cipollone in Pittsburgh, Pennsylvania, has provided a format for a resume.

Reproducible 7-1

RESUME MAKER

BASIC HEADINGS

- Name and Contact Information (including e-mail)
- Objective
- Education and Training
- Skills and Accomplishments
- Employment History
- Hobbies and Interests
- References

NAME/CONTACT INFORMATION

At the top of your resume, you should include your *name, address, telephone number (cell phone and home number [if you have one])*, and *e-mail address.* E-mail address should sound and look professional: first initial, last name, number; for example, **lbrown2025@email.com**.

OBJECTIVE

State what you want to achieve regarding employment. *Select one* objective from the following and feel free to change it to how it fits you.

- To obtain a position that will utilize my skills and education in the field of _____.
- To obtain a position that will utilize my education and skills while I am attending college.
- Seeking a position with opportunity for growth and advancement.
- High school student seeking position that will allow for growth within company.
- High school student seeking position for summer employment.

  Other examples:
- Short-term goal: to obtain entry-level experience; long-term goals: to become a teacher, doctor, police officer, and more.

SELECT ONLY *ONE* OBJECTIVE

EDUCATION AND TRAINING

Start with the Years you will be in High School ONLY: 2020–2025. Type out: Happy Valley High School; Graduation: June 2025

National Honor Society, Volunteer in office/library, Student Council, cheerleading, Church Choir, football/basketball team, and so on.

SKILLS AND ACCOMPLISHMENTS

Skills are what you are good at naturally or have learned. Skills will increase your earning power financially. If you have a skill such as taking great photographs or making websites, this will increase your earning power with your employer if they have a need for this type of service.

Achievements may be things you did with others or alone at a job or in school if you never had a job. If you have no achievement, you may want to start acquiring some. Listen to the bulletin @ lunchtime for opportunities.

Examples of Skills

- Computer skills include Microsoft Office: Word and PowerPoint
- Internet research and e-mail
- Ability to get along with others
- Able to work independently and without supervision
- Able to lift over 100 lbs.

Examples of Accomplishments

- Coordinated after-school program for neighborhood children
- Persuaded principal to recycle trash in the cafeteria
- Responsible for keeping bookshelves clean in the library
- Trained new employees at my workplace
- Trained new players on my sports team
- Wrote an article for the school newspaper
- Student-Council Member

Reproducible 7-1 (*Continued*)

WORK EXPERIENCE

List only jobs that you had for more than two months and do not "embellish." Always tell the truth. List your latest job first. Put the month and year: 03/2020.

Keep your work responsibilities brief. Use phrases: kept kitchen clean at all times, assisted children with after-school activities, responsible for making meals per order in restaurant, responsible for feeding and keeping child safe while babysitting, and so on.

HOBBIES/INTERESTS

Since you have little work experience, by providing hobbies and/or interests, you will let the employer know a little bit about your personality and character. Use positive phrases, and list things that show skills that could be employable, such as enjoying sewing, playing sports, cooking dinner for my family, listening to music, playing a musical instrument, reading, gardening, cleaning my mother's car, and so on.

REFERENCES

If you have specific references, list them. Try not to use relatives unless you worked for them, such as helping your grandmother around the house. When listing references, put name, title, or relationship to you (teacher, nurse, neighbor, or relative), and put their address and phone number.

ALWAYS PROVIDE ACCURATE AND TRUTHFUL INFORMATION—IF NOT, YOU COULD POSSIBLY BE FIRED.

Other items in your job-seeking corner will include the want ads section from the local newspaper with job ads and also housing opportunities as well as online bookmarks or "hot lists" of job-seeking online resources. You can add the information from the financial literacy section to help students calculate just what it will cost for them to live on their own and give them some indication of the amount of take-home pay they will need just to survive. Other more in-depth information is discussed in the next section, which is for those students who have made a decision to go directly from high school to a job.

High School to Job

Those who plan to look for a job as soon as they graduate will need the same type of information as the school leaver, so these students will also make use of your job-seeking corner. Be sure that you have updated the information here at least once a semester to make sure everything is accurate and up to date. Asking a student assistant or other students to help identify resources to add or update can help you both. Students who themselves use the information should be able to point out any inaccuracies, or they may ask questions that will lead you to recognize the need to update your information. Having it all in electronic format makes corrections and updating easy.

At this point, students are aware that finding a job will take time unless they began that process before graduation. The guidance counselors working with the librarian can gather job ads that will be appropriate for students to apply. The writing skills taught throughout will be used to write the cover letter for the job application. Students will have had opportunities to practice interviewing for a job; again it happens with the guidance counselor and teachers helping with this process. It might even be appropriate for people in the community to come into the school to help students practice their interviewing skills. The more they practice, the less difficult it is in that real world.

Apprenticeships

Students who will be continuing their education beyond high school may be looking for opportunities to learn a trade. The U.S. Department of Labor website states,

> If you are interested in exploring apprenticeship as the next step in your career, there are many ways to find opportunities in your area. Many businesses advertise their apprenticeship openings in local media and commercial job search sites. You can also access apprenticeships through your local American Job Center; often, American Job Centers partner with local businesses to match job-seekers with available opportunities. You can find the telephone number and location of the nearest American Job Center by typing in your ZIP code using the search tool at https://www.careeronestop.org/site/american-job -center.aspx.

You can also access listings of apprenticeship opportunities by using the Apprenticeship Finder Tool or by contacting your state apprenticeship agency. (https://www.dol.gov/apprenticeship/)

Apprenticeships offer paychecks from the day you go to work and increase over time as you begin working on the job. In many cases, your employer will support your further education and the ability to earn college credit, perhaps earning that associate or bachelor's degree.

Beauty and Barber Colleges and Trade Schools

Graduates who want practical training for a profession will have a good idea of what the trade or technical schools near them will be like because representatives from these schools have come to the high school one or more evenings when students and parents can ask questions about the time commitment and cost of classes and what students will be able to do and the kinds of jobs they can apply for when they have completed their training. Students may be able to enroll in some classes before they graduate, getting a start toward completing their coursework about the same time as students going to universities will have taken Advanced Placement classes.

Your graduates need to understand they will be facing their new environment, new type of training, and new studies, and they may find themselves in a classroom with a much larger number of students. The individual attention given to them in a high school is lost when the teachers/trainers have larger numbers of students to teach. In the case of trade and technical schools, instruction is directly related to the work that they will specifically be doing. The schedule of classes may be much different than that in high school when an entire day is devoted to instruction and practice in a single area.

Students who wish to become beauticians or barbers will find opportunities in locations sometimes called beauty colleges or academies and barber colleges. The time to complete the course varies widely. Some trade schools are two-year college programs that offer courses for students who want to increase their skills in business, finance, hospitality, construction, engineering, graphic or other visual arts, and computer or information technology. Some offer these short programs for health care personnel, such as dental assistants. Graduates will need to be prepared to meet the cost of the tuition for any of these training institutions and to understand that if they do not complete the program, their effort and their tuition will have been for nothing.

Community College and Four-Year Institutions

Community college and four-year institutions, with their different schedules to meet, can be challenging during that first semester. Those students who want to work and go to school may take fewer classes, which can be scheduled in the evenings. When they are full-time students, their schedules may include one course three mornings a week and another course three afternoons a week, with other courses meeting on the other two days. When coursework includes a lab session, this must be scheduled so they do not overlap with the lecture sessions. Having a recent high school graduate return to your school can explain some of this to your students. Or you can do this with an evening session including parents with their children.

Community colleges provide both programs that earn students a credential to go to work and the first two years of college before moving to a four-year institution. At the community college and university, students need to know that they are expected to take total responsibility for their learning. Most students will be paying tuition to be able to attend class, and if a failed course must be retaken, tuition is assessed as if the student has never taken the course before. Students who do not succeed over time are asked to leave the college or university, and all funds paid to the university are a total loss. To meet the educational obligations, students need to understand before they apply for this training that they must get their assignments in on time and at a degree that meets what the faculty member has determined is a passing level.

Attending college classes is the best method to learn the content of the class, and similar to high school, students should have read the assigned reading before coming to class. At this level, it may seem easier just to skip class if one has not prepared for the lecture. In high school, the school office will make a call if a student is not in class. At the college level, this is not done. Students who miss class are expected to find out about the content and make up anything they have missed on their own.

It is more challenging than high school because the responsibility for keeping up with assignments and meeting deadlines falls squarely on the shoulders of the student. Forgetting or ignoring deadlines is not something to try to negotiate later. While students in college may be assigned a counselor, that person will not be acting in a custodial capacity and will not have much time to spend on a failing student who is not attending class or turning in assignments on time.

Once at the school, the competition for grades is different, and this is something you can share with your students so it does not surprise them. Many of the students in any freshman class were in the top 10 percent of their classes in high school; in this new environment, 100 percent of the competition is very similar to the graduates of your high school; they are used to working hard, studying late, and vying for those top grades. For most, this is a new and usually unexpected competition among fellow students, and it can be devastating if they are not warned before they arrive at their freshman orientation.

Graduates who leave home for a distant college, particularly if they are first-generation students to go to college, become a part of a new environment with some similarities but many differences in where they live, get their meals, and make and meet new friends. Students who may have gone with their parents to visit the campus before the application process to decide which applications to send may have a sense of the campus and may have visited the dormitories and have some idea of what they will be like. For many students, visiting college campuses was not possible; their choice was made with the availability of financial aid from the school. Many colleges help meet this challenge by finding alumni in the area to talk with the student. If this does not seem to be happening, you can try to find someone who attended the school who can talk about the campus and campus life.

Universities have different ways to assign roommates to dormitory rooms, and the numbers sharing bedrooms and bathrooms may be quite different from a student's home. If counselors have helped students during the application process, they may have recommended that if students can afford to do so, go for a weekend to see exactly what the dormitory is like when school is in session. Sharing is a part of the process, and perhaps some of this could be helped if high school graduates who are home for a vacation could come to the library and talk about their experiences.

As more and more organizations offer education and training online, many graduates will be able to do so in an online environment. Some may have graduated from high schools where at least one online experience is required for graduation, while for others, it will be a new and different way to go to school. Not only is online learning used for college class instruction but many will also encounter it as webinars needed for their work or distance learning to acquire new skills within their job.

From an apprenticeship to a four-year academic program, your graduates will be meeting coworkers and bosses, other students, and new faculty. These may have a very different view of working and learning, and with all, there is a different price to that schooling. It is no longer free as is public education in the United States. Continuing in the program means working at the best of one's ability to gain the most from the experience, whether being paid in an apprenticeship or paying tuition at another institution for the privilege of learning.

Interpersonal Relations

One must face so many new realizations upon entering a new environment with a totally different group: new employers and employees in the workplace and new teachers and students in education programs. Many of these realizations become interpersonal challenges. The new work environment requires arriving at work, completing assigned tasks in a manner acceptable to those in charge, and carrying out assigned responsibilities in a timely fashion. This can make the difference between continued employment and the need to look for a new job lacking a recommendation letter. The workplace does not offer a study hall to catch up on work; at best, an employee has a 15-minute coffee break in the morning and afternoon. Places of employment anticipate a good performance, sometimes with very little direct instruction. The new student, whether trade school or college, may often begin with little sense of what is expected.

In college, new students navigate their new environment with little help beyond a general orientation session at the beginning of the semester. They need your help to find as much information available about their choice, including what and whom to ask if they have questions or problems. Their first hurdle may be when they arrive at the residence hall and need the key to their room, which was in the instructions they left at home. This may include finding the college health facility before they are ill and finding any college-tutoring department the minute they feel they are not keeping up with their work. It is always better to have these before they are needed than to try to find them in a crisis situation. They also need to know about the services of the placement office so they can begin to gather information for their resume long before their senior year when they begin their job search in earnest.

Find examples of those people they will encounter, including employers, staff, faculty, and college students who can come into your library, and point out the reality of getting along in their worlds. The examples may include a boss who will discuss how performance is judged and the result of those judgments. Provide some information about the working atmosphere and getting along with coworkers in that setting. Students who are going on for additional training or education need to hear about how to pick a suitable plan for completing the degree, attending their required classes or training sessions, and the problems associated with missing any of these, behavior that is their new individual responsibility for learning.

> When offering a workshop about life after graduation, you could invite parents who faced this three or more years earlier with their own children. Ask them to share their original views of continuing responsibility to children after graduation and if they have changed. With children who have remained living at home either to work or to attend a course, is it still "under my roof, under my rules," or have they graduated to complete freedom for coming and going? Are those working expected to share in household costs, including part of any automobile expenses?

Interpersonal relations come into play with that roommate. If the roommate is someone who rises early in the morning, this will probably upset the sleep of the night owl who likes to work until 2:00 a.m. and then sleep late. While most universities place athletes in the same dormitory, if they do not, the early and late practices may affect those not on the team. It is all a part of learning how to get along with others.

Time-management decisions were previously orchestrated by parents who reminded their children to do their homework and teachers who gave deadlines for the submission of assignments often with frequent reminders of those due dates. Suddenly making sure the rent and utilities are paid and arranging study time so that coursework is completed rest squarely on the shoulders of this new adult. These discussions should happen before leaving high school because it is less likely someone will be there to help resolve these issues after graduation. Many of them have financial consequences.

Financial Consequences of Decisions

Financial consequences evolve with almost every decision in our lives, and your graduates need to consider what their salary figure actually means. It will have deductions that may greatly reduce the actual take-home pay. In addition, they need to take into account what that net salary will actually cover, where the new employee will live, whom to live with, how to read a contract carefully before signing it, the actual cost of credit card debt, which bank has the best rates, and managing debt and especially how to pay back loans for purchases and education. Your financial literacy programs and activities throughout their school years will help them with decisions at this time.

For those going immediately to work or going to training or beginning at a local college may choose to and be welcome to stay at home. This may seem an easier solution than it really is. Siblings may have been poised to move into a room as soon as the older sibling has moved out. Parents may consider the graduate still a child rather than an adult and may insist upon rules and regulations that were in place before rather than understand the need for independence. Parents may also anticipate that if their graduate is living at home, some payment for the privilege of room and board is expected. These types of issues need discussion; for graduates to acknowledge their obligation of pay for some expenses while living at home will show parents that they are assuming a more adult role. They can find out what rental costs are and estimate what their portion of the family food costs would be. If they are using a family car for transportation, what portion of the gasoline, repairs, and insurance costs would be theirs? This will give them a starting figure to try to be more independent.

If the graduate plans to move away from home to be out on his or her own, or when the potential job is not local, he or she needs to look at newspaper ads and online sources to locate places to live and the requirements to move in, such as prepayment of a month's rent and a deposit for damages or only that first month's rent. Together, these may represent a large expenditure when no salary has yet been earned. These budget considerations may affect the decision to remain at home or move out or to turn down a job in another location because the salary will not cover the living expenses for the move. One option is to plan to share an apartment.

Deciding to share an apartment means finding a roommate. This may seem a lark after all those sleepovers and weekend experiences, but even a good friend can have interesting long-term habits not realized in the social world of high school. An ad may specify it is a shared situation, and the person writing the ad will probably be the person "in charge" of selecting the person to share. Creating a list of the estimated expenses of sharing an apartment should be joined with a list of the expectations. New graduates need to consider their requirements if they are going to share and what would not be a good situation: how much clutter is acceptable, who does the cleaning, who does the cooking as well as cleaning up after meals (shared or singly prepared), and who is going to be a frequent guest and how long is the visit? Also, discussions should point out ways to get out of a difficult situation, something that is never easy, and how costly this might become.

Credit card companies spend enormous sums of advertising money encouraging young people to get a credit card. They make it look very easy to get the card, and it is. They may even offer a free enrollment year to get that person signed onto the card and even ignore the cost of having the card for the next year. It is not a happy situation to find that just to have that card may have a fee that is sizeable. Credit card companies never announce just how quickly someone can create a sizeable debt. The interest rate for credit card debt often finds the person able to cover only the interest on the card and the debt is not reduced. Teaching the financial pitfalls of credit cards has been discussed in previous chapters, and this information should be taught throughout high school; it is a necessity. The credit card debt in the United States is extremely high, and students need to learn the pitfalls of a credit card before they sign up and long before they experience the reality about that annual charge and the interest rate on unpaid balances.

Helping students learn about the checking accounts would be best done by asking a bank teller to come to school with this information. If the interested group meets in the library to discuss the questions they will have, some of comparative research can determine similar services at other banks before the speaker arrives. This will show how to look at differences so that their questions can address substantive issues. A bank employee will confirm the information they find, such as the minimum amounts to be in the account for free checking or the cost of writing each check, how to handle a checking account app on a phone, and paying bills by automatic withdrawal, among other things. If banks do have major differences in services, they will have the opportunity to ask someone who will know some of the reasons why.

The real world for all has all kinds of contracts, and these have small print that must be given close attention. Persons who have new jobs and new apartments need to be very careful to read the lease agreement for where they are living, just as college students who are allowed to live off campus rather than in the dormitories must be able to determine exactly what that lease says are the tenants' responsibilities. Any problems with walls, rooms, appliances, and furniture need to be pointed out before the lease is signed so that no charges are assessed when moving out of the apartment. Losing the front-door key can be a major challenge when it is time to go home for the summer.

The student who must borrow money to pay for trade schools or college costs for tuition and housing may find that repayment beginning immediately when they graduate. Beginning salaries even for professionals are at the bottom of the scale and may challenge the ability to cover that college loan as quickly as one would like. Few opportunities allow for any reduction although in some states and for some professionals such as a teacher, or a physician who agrees to practice in a rural area, there may be a reduction for some of the loan for that college loan. If students leave school before graduating, they may find that their loan comes due immediately too. When they leave school without the degree, they may not be able to find a job that pays enough to repay the loan, and these loans do not go away.

If you can help students and parents research this aspect of the decision to borrow money to attend any further training, they may be able to accept a delay in starting school when they are considering whether to try to earn money before beginning school or if they can get a part-time job to help with their expenses and still make their obligations as a student. While working to save money before going to college or working while attending college means it may take a little longer to graduate, but it lowers the amount of any debt when they do graduate.

Becoming Good Citizens: Decision Consequences

One of the greatest feelings of students when they walk off that stage with their diplomas in hand is that they are, in fact, adults, and for most, the world is literally their oyster—the independence that comes with this realization that they are on their own, ready to leave home, and out from under their parents' watchful eye. Freedom without restraint can have some long-lasting and critical outcomes if rules that make for good citizenship are not honored.

Finding information about those rules comes from those next-step locations. If it is a job, those rules include some orientation to time to arrive, check in or punch a time clock, where to dress if a uniform is required, and a tour of the facility with any hazards to avoid. Information sent by the community colleges and the universities helps students with knowledge about arriving on campus and moving into housing, where to park a car if you can have a car on campus, and hours of the cafeteria and library, among many others. Providing a time and place for students to bring information about their school choices into the library will allow them to compare notes with others about different locations and give all an opportunity to discuss ways to meet these rules.

Most higher education institutions have few rules and regulations, but most have a grade point average their students must maintain to remain at the school. Students need this information to decide how many courses they can realistically enroll in for any given semester.

Good citizens exercise good judgment all the time. This good judgment may be threatened and even replaced by the need to be a part of the crowd, and the decision to become a part of that crowd may mean being involved in some out-of-control happening where those who participated were dismissed from a job or a training program or a university. It is never easy to convince young adults that they can be caught off guard in a situation that can accelerate to a disaster. You and the guidance counselor could hold lunch-hour or even after-school small group discussions of potential situations and possible outcomes from different settings and possible reactions.

Participating in a democracy requires being a good citizen and helping elect candidates for office at all levels. One may choose a party to join or just register to vote as an independent. Every 18-year-old should register to vote. You can encourage teachers who teach seniors to mention this in classes or even go into classes with voter registrations in hand, mentioning that right after class you will be there ready and willing to help them fill out that form. Helping their children register to vote and celebrating afterward could be a birthday gift for parents to give their children. The library should have the information about the locations to go register to vote or have forms on hand and post this information all year. It should become a goal of every high school student. Information about voting as an absentee voter should be given to all students, but particularly to those students who are going away to college so that they are able to vote in every election.

Many states have made it even easier to vote by mail. Students who maintain their home addresses where they were living when they went to school can request an absentee ballot. Or those who are still in their community may want to request a mail-in ballot so they do not have to go before or after work. The goal is to become citizens who vote in every election, including those off-year elections for offices such as school boards, as well as the primaries and presidential elections. Many states put propositions or bond issues on the ballot that decide other things in our lives.

It is not easy to discuss comparison of candidates and still maintain neutrality with elections; yet, students need to think about what they have learned from their parents and how that affects what they think about parties and platforms. Good citizens must understand the issues facing them whether electing a candidate or supporting an issue before a city council or a school board meeting.

When you are teaching information literacy skills, you constantly evaluate your students' abilities to find answers to their questions in appropriate sources and anticipate that your students will detect false facts and question the validity of all news. This senior year is the time to make that final effort to send graduates out with the ability to find information and the desire to test information for its authenticity as well as to instill in those soon-to-be graduates the desire to continue their learning through their lifetimes. For those going to another institution, explain the difference between the Dewey decimal classification system and Library of Congress system. Both have numbers that are addresses for the books on the shelves, and their new library may have some of the same databases that you have provided for them, but they may have many new and different resources. Encourage them to go to the library for any tours available for freshmen in case their teachers are not offering this as a part of their course. Becoming familiar with the library will be a place to study as well as a place to find information.

Reminding them of all the resources available in their public libraries has been a constant "lesson" throughout their years in school. They need to remember the value of that library at all points in their lives.

Raising the question "Have students been taught what they need to meet their civic responsibilities?" the Brown Center Report states,

> We turn to what appears to be as close as we could reasonably expect to a consensus view from experts—the Six Proven Practices for Effective Civic Learning framework. Motivating this framework is a notion that teaching students facts about U.S. government is a goal, but not the exclusive goal, of civics education. The ultimate aim is a more comprehensive and interactive understanding of civics. Specifically, the framework proposes three key components:
>
> 1. Civic knowledge: an understanding of government structure, government processes, and relevant social studies knowledge and concepts
>
> 2. Civic skills: abilities that enable students to participate in a democracy as responsible citizens; and
>
> 3. Civic dispositions: attitudes important in a democracy such as a sense of civic duty and concern for the welfare of others
>
> Together, these components of civics education equip individuals to participate in our democratic system.[1]

Have all graduates gained the understanding that they have a responsibility to do all that they can to sustain our democracy? They need to learn and keep fresh their knowledge of the issues facing their cities, counties, states, and the nation. It is not a case of hoping someone else will take the responsibility and fix everything for them. They are essential to this process, and that means voting and encouraging others to vote, working when necessary for legislation needed to fix problems. It may mean running for office, and that may be the ultimate political decision. Before that, they can work for persons they feel should be elected. Citizenship includes joining in community events, being on juries, and finding ways to connect with neighbors to build safe neighborhoods.

School librarians who have spent time helping students find information to help them succeed as students while they are in the building as well as to choose their next steps in life may wonder what to do when they have left that school. With the ease of social media, continuing your role as that "go-to" person will not be difficult. It will be a compliment to you and your efforts to prepare them if they continue to ask your opinion about their questions if they have difficulty solving their problems after they have left the school. This acknowledges your leadership in providing information and experiences in the school that helped them understand those things not necessarily taught in the classroom but essential in their lives after high school.

Activities

1. If students who come to you indicating they are going to drop out of school consider you to be a trustworthy adult, you may be able to find out the real reason behind this decision. When it is the difficulties of the course load, the guidance counselor may have suggestions for a different course. Problems at home may need to be reported to legal authorities. Whatever the reason, anyone leaving high school before graduation should consider the following:

   Are parents and other caregivers aware of the situation?

   What other options have they considered?

   What to do to replace the missing diploma?

   Who is available to help them when they need help of any kind?

2. Students who complete their resumes could bring those to a scheduled lunch session where they are reviewed by other students, teachers, or community members who can help them improve these.

3. One way to help students imagine themselves in a place they might be living in the future is to have them go to the website of their future location of the town they might like to live in. Ask them to locate several places such as the library, hospital(s), churches, shops, and recreation facilities, among others. You can brainstorm these places as a group first. Have them create a "day in the life" and where they would go and what they would do. Allow enough time for them to share this fantasy with others via projection. Let them brainstorm ways to get around or other ideas of things to do should they go live in that town. The sharing is important; it can get discussion going, and suggestions will come by looking at the map and identifying places that have unfamiliar names. Check them out to see what the website tells about this place.

4. A campus map of one or more institutions where students are planning to attend can allow them to look at the relationship of dorms to classrooms, the stadium and field house, and other recreation facilities, such as a swimming pool and cafeteria. If the campus has a union building, what activities are housed there? Students should be

able to locate the health center, the buildings where their classes will be held, and any transportation offered around campus or to campus from distant dormitories.

5. A small group discussion at lunch hour or at the end of the school day can give students an opportunity to pose scenarios and then discuss outcomes. While this is the assignment of the guidance counselor, students may prefer to hold this session on their own. Some possibilities include the following:

- You need a part-time job to help with expenses.

- You and your roommate are at a party, and your roommate has had too much alcohol.

- You are out late at night after a class and have to get back to your dorm. It is the end of the month, and you just spent your last dollar.

- You just had a huge fight with your roommate.

- Your date turns out to be not what or who you expected.

- You woke up late for class.

- You are invited to a frat party where they are serving alcohol against university rules.

- Your roommate's date does not seem to be leaving, and it is really late.

- A football player who regularly misses class asks you for your notes.

- Your professor seems too friendly with students and asks you to make an appointment.

Note

1. Michael Hansen, Elizabeth Mann Levesque, Jon Valant, and Diana Quintero, *The 2018 Brown Center Report on American Education: How Well Are American Students Learning?* Brown Center on Education Policy at Brookings, June 2018, p. 16, accessed July 23, 2018, https://www.brookings.edu/multi-chapter-report/the-2018-brown-center-report-on-american-education/.

Bibliography

ABC-CLIO. "American Government." https://www.abc-clio.com/ABC-CLIOCorporate/product.aspx?pc=AGOAW.

Abilock, Debbie, Kristin Fontichiaro, and Violet H. Harada, eds. *Growing Schools: Librarians as Professional Developers*. Santa Barbara, CA: Libraries Unlimited, 2012.

Achterman, Doug. "MAD." E-mail message. June 10, 2018.

ACLU. "Meeting with Your Elected Representatives." https://www.aclu.org/meeting-your-elected-representatives.

American Association of School Librarians. *National School Library Standards: For Learners, School Librarians, and School Libraries*. Chicago, IL: ALA Editions, 2018.

American Library Association. "Importance of Play." ALSC. Last modified 2018. Accessed August 6, 2018. http://www.ala.org/alsc/publications-resources/white-papers/importance-play.

American Library Association. "Library Bill of Rights." Issues and Advocacy. Accessed July 1, 2018. http://www.ala.org/advocacy/intfreedom/librarybill.

American Speech-Language-Hearing Association. "Meeting with Your Members of Congress Locally." https://www.asha.org/Advocacy/grassroots/Visiting-Your-Local-Congressional-Office/.

Annoyed Librarian. "Life Lessons @ Your Library." *Library Journal* (blog). May 22, 2013. Accessed August 6, 2018. https://lj.libraryjournal.com/blogs/annoyedlibrarian/2013/05/22/life-lessons-your-library/.

Barco, Kathy, and Melanie Borski-Howard. *Storytime and Beyond: Having Fun with Early Literacy*. Santa Barbara, CA: Libraries Unlimited, 2018.

Barr, Donald A. "When Trauma Hinders Learning." *Phi Delta Kappan* 99 (February 2018): 44.

Bender, Melinda. "Open House in the Library." E-mail message. May 9, 2018.

Ben's Guide to the U.S. Government. https://bensguide.gpo.gov/.

Bierman, Karen, Mark Greenberg, and Rachel Abenavoli. *Promoting Social and Emotional Learning in Preschool—Programs and Practices That Work*. State College, PA: Pennsylvania State University, Edna Bennett Pierce Prevention Research Center, 2017.

Bruel, Nick. *Bad Kitty for President*. Square Fish, 2012.

Bruening, Kim. "Who's the Boss?" 2012. Accessed August 6, 2018. https://www.kshs.org/teachers/professional/pdfs/bruening_whos_boss.pdf.

Bureau of Labor Statistics. *Occupational Outlook Handbook*. Last modified April 13, 2018. https://www.bls.gov/ooh/.

Cardinali, Emily. "What Your State Is Doing to Beef Up Civics Education." July 21, 2018. Accessed July 24, 2018. https://www.npr.org/sections/ed/2018/07/21/624267576/what-your -state-is-doing-to-beef-up-civics-education.

Career Cruising. https://public.careercruising.com/en/.

CareerOneStop. http://www.acinet.org/.

CareerOneStop. "Find an American Job Center." https://www.careeronestop.org/site/american-job -center.aspx.

"Career Spotlight." YouTube. Posted by USA.gov. December 23, 2016. Accessed August 6, 2018. https://www.youtube.com/playlist?list=PLDB4BCE9817AE7B43.

Career Zone. www.cacareerzone.org.

Carroll, Joyce Armstrong, Kelley Barger, Karla James, and Kristy Hill. *Guided by Meaning in Primary Literacy: Libraries, Reading, Writing, and Learning*. Santa Barbara, CA: Libraries Unlimited, 2016.

Chang, Alisa. "How to Meet Your Congressman." NPR *Morning Edition*. March 26, 2014. https://www.npr.org/2014/3/26/294361018/how-to-meet-your-congressman.

Christiansen, Candace. *The Mitten Tree*. Golden, CO: Fulcrum Publishing, 2009.

Civic Action Project: Constitutional Rights Foundation. http://www.crfcap.org/mod/page/view .php?id=206.

Clanton, Ben. *Vote for Me!* Boston, MA: Kids Can Press. 2012.

College Board. "Daily Practice for the New SAT." SAT Suite of Assessments. https:// collegereadiness.collegeboard.org/sat/practice/daily-practice-app.

Constitution Day Poster Contest. https://www.constitutionfacts.com/constitution-poster-design -contest/.

Court, Joy. *Read to Succeed: Strategies to Engage Children and Young People in Reading for Pleasure*. London: Facet Publishing, 2011.

Court, Joy. *Reading by Right: Successful Strategies to Ensure Every Child Can Read to Success*. London: Facet Publishing, 2017.

Cronin, Doreen. *Duck for President*. A Click-Clack Book. New York: Atheneum Books, 2004.

"Data Point: Early High School Dropouts: What Are Their Characteristics?" U.S. Department of Education. February 2015. http://nces.ed.gov/surveys/hsls09.

Dawkins, April. "Overdue Fees: Barriers to Access in School Libraries." *Intellectual Freedom Blog*. October 12, 2017. Accessed August 6, 2018. https://www.oif.ala.org/oif/?p=10955.

Deskins, Liz, and Christina H. Dorr. *Linking Picture Books to National Content Standards: 200+ Lives to Explore*. Santa Barbara, CA: Libraries Unlimited, 2015.

EBSCO. https://www.ebsco.com/products/research-databases/vocational-career-collection.

Education Planner. "Start Thinking about Life after High School." http://www.educationplanner .org.

Ehrenreich, Barbara. *Nickel and Dimed: On (Not) Getting By in America*. London: Picador, 2012.

FDIC. "Money Smart for Young People Grades 6–8." Accessed August 6, 2018. https://catalog .fdic.gov/money-smart-young-people-grades-6-8-downloadable.

First 5 California. http://www.first5california.com/learning-center.aspx?lang=en&id=11.

First 5 California: Guessing Game. http://www.first5california.com/activity-center.aspx?id= 18&sub=81.

Gale's Career Online High School. http://www.careeronlinehs.gale.com/.

Gale's Career Transitions. https://www.gale.com/c/career-transitions.

Gooch, C. Kay, and Charlotte Massey. *Camp Summer Read: How to Create Your Own Summer Reading Camp*. Santa Barbara, CA: Libraries Unlimited, 2010.

Guccione, Bob, Jr. "Signs of the Times." *Spin* (July 1991): 58–62, 91–92.

Hannigan, Kate. *A Lady Has the Floor: Belva Lockwood Speaks Out for Women's Rights*. Honesdale, PA: Calkins Creek, 2018.

Hansen, Michael, Elizabeth Mann Levesque, Jon Valant, and Diana Quintero. *The 2018 Brown Center Report on American Education: How Well Are American Students Learning?* Brown Center on Education Policy at Brookings. June 2018. Accessed July 23, 2018. https://www.brookings.edu/multi-chapter-report/the-2018-brown-center-report-on-american-education/.

Hobbs, Nancy, Kristen Sacco, and Myra R. Oleynik. *Personalized Reading: It's a Piece of PIE*. Santa Barbara, CA: Libraries Unlimited, 2010.

Hough, Brenda. *Crash Course in Time Management for Library Staff*. Santa Barbara, CA: Libraries Unlimited, 2018.

Housing a Forest. "Simple American Flag Craft for Kids." June 17, 2014. http://www.housingaforest.com/simple-american-flag-craft-for-kids/.

The Humane Society of the United States. "How to Start a Club." http://www.humanesociety.org/about/departments/students/clubs/how_to_start_a_club.html.

iCivics. https://www.icivics.org/.

Kennedy, Frances. *The Pickle Patch Bathtub*. Berkeley, CA: Tricycle Press, 2004.

Klaus, Peggy. *Brag! The Art of Tooting Your Own Horn without Blowing It*. New York: Warner Business Books, 2004.

Krashen, Stephen. *Free Voluntary Reading*. Santa Barbara, CA: Libraries Unlimited, 2011.

Krashen, Stephen. *The Power of Reading: Insights from the Research*. 2nd ed. Westport, CT: Libraries Unlimited, 2004.

Krashen, Stephen, Sy-Ying Lee, and Christy Lao. *Comprehensive and Compelling: The Causes and Effects of Free Voluntary Reading*. Santa Barbara, CA: Libraries Unlimited, 2018.

Kuhlthau, Carol C., Leslie K. Maniotes, and Ann K. Caspari. *Guided Inquiry Design®: A Framework for Inquiry in Your School*. Santa Barbara, CA: Libraries Unlimited, 2012.

Life Works: Explore Health and Medical Science Careers. http://www.science.education.nih.gov/Lifeworks.

Maryland Radio Network. *The First Five Years*. http://wypr.org/programs/first-five-years.

McNeil, Heather. *Read, Rhyme, and Romp: Early Literacy Skills and Activities for Librarians, Teachers, and Parents*. Santa Barbara, CA: Libraries Unlimited, 2012.

Mitchell, Amy, Jeffrey Gottfried, Michael Barthel, and Elisa Shearer. "Pathway to News." Pew Research Center Journalism and Media. Last modified July 7, 2016. Accessed July 1, 2018. http://www.journalism.org/2016/07/07/pathways-to-news/.

Mother Goose on the Loose. https:www.mgol.net/.

National Anthems Channel. https://www.youtube.com/user/NationalAnthemsChan.

National Archives and Records Administration. "Our Documents." The People's Vote. https://www.ourdocuments.gov/index.php?flash=true&.

National Constitution Center. "American Flag Pinwheels." https://constitutioncenter.org/media/files/American_Flag_Pinwheels.pdf.

National Council of Teachers of English. "Visiting Your Legislator in Washington, DC." www.ncte.org/action/reqappt.

National Park Service. NPS.gov.

O*Net. *Occupational Outlook Handbook*. http://online.netcenter.org/skills/.

Our Documents. https://www.ourdocuments.gov/index.php?flash=true&.

Pew Research Center. "Newspapers Fact Sheet." Pew Research Center Journalism and Media. Last modified June 13, 2018. Accessed July 1, 2018. http://www.journalism.org/fact-sheet/newspapers/.

Pew Research Center. "Social Media Fact Sheet." Pew Research Center Internet and Technology. Last modified February 5, 2018. Accessed July 1, 2018. http://www.pewinternet.org/fact-sheet/social-media/.

Presidents Song. https://www.youtube.com/results?search_query=presidents+song+for+kids.

ProQuest. Career & Technical Education Database. https://www.proquest.com/products-services/pq_career_tech_ed.html.

Richard Myles Johnson Foundation. http://www.rmjfoundation.org/index.php/bite-of-reality.

Right Question Institute. http://www.rightquestion.org.

Rosen Digital. Financial Literacy. Last modified 2018. Accessed August 6, 2018. http://financialliteracy.rosendigital.com/.

Ross, Catherine Sheldrick, Lynne (E. F.) McKechnie, and Paulette M. Rothbauer. *Reading Still Matters: What the Research Reveals about Reading, Libraries, and Community*. Santa Barbara, CA: Libraries Unlimited, 2018.

Rothstein, Dan, and Liz Santana. *Make Just One Change: Teach Students to Ask Their Own Questions*. Boston, MA: Harvard Education Press, 2011.

Sanders, Rob. *Pride: The Story of Harvey Mudd and the Rainbow Flag*. New York: Random House, 2018.

"Sandra Day O'Connor Quotes." BrainyQuote. Last modified 2018. https://www.brainyquote.com/quotes/sandra_day_oconnor_471730.

SCORE. https://www.score.org/.

Sessler, John, and Connie Williams. "Asking Questions in the Age of Google." Lecture. November 2017. Accessed July 14, 2018. https://www.ebsco.com/blog/article/asking-questions-in-the-age-of-google-webinar-recap.

Soderlund, Ashley. "The Surprising Reason Your Child Is Suddenly Cranky (and What to Do about It)." *Nurture and Thrive* (blog). 2016. https://nurtureandthriveblog.com/the-surprising-reason-your-child-is-suddenly-cranky-and-what-to-do-about-it/.

Sorenson, Karen Sue. "Open House in the Library." E-mail. June 9, 2018.

Sparks, Sarah D. "How the Humble Lemonade Stand Is Becoming a Pipeline for Young Entrepreneurs." *Education Week*. July 29, 2018.

St. George, Judith. *So You Want to Be President*. New York: Philomel Books, 2000.

Teacher-Directed Activities. *Many Ways to Win*. https://www.msjc.edu/cte/Documents/MWTW-Teacher-Directed-Activities%20MSJC.pdf.

Texas Workforce Commission. "Careers Are Everywhere." Labor Market and Career Information. Accessed August 6, 2018. https://lmci.state.tx.us/shared/CareersAreEverywhere.asp.

TreasuryDirect. "Money Math: Lessons for Life." https://www.treasurydirect.gov/indiv/tools/tools_moneymath.htm.

U.S. Department of Labor. Employment and Training Administration (ETA). "State Contact List." Apprenticeship. Last modified April 3, 2018. Accessed August 6, 2018. https://www.doleta.gov/OA/contactlist.cfm.

U.S. Landmarks. https://www.pinterest.com/search/pins/?q=u.s.%20landmarks&rs=typed.

U.S. Mint. https://www.usmint.gov/learn/kids.

USA.gov. "How to Contact Your Elected Officials." https://www.usa.gov/elected-officials.

Vermont State Treasurer. http://secure2.vermonttreasurer.gov/legacywebsite/www.vermonttreasurer
.gov/sites/treasurer/files/pdf/literacy/2012%20Kindergarten%20Pickle.pdf.

Visa. "Peter Pig's Money Counter." Practical Money Skills. Last modified 2018. Accessed August 6,
2018. https://practicalmoneyskills.com/play/peter_pigs_money_counter.

Volkman, John D. *Collaborative Research Projects: Inquiry That Stimulates the Senses*. Westport,
CT: Libraries Unlimited, 2008.

Williams, Connie. "From School to Community: Inspiring Student Activism." *School Library Connection*. May/June 2018.

Williams, Connie. *Got Civics? Knowledge Quest* (blog). June 2018. https://knowledgequest.aasl.org/
author/cwilliams/.

Willingham, Daniel T. *Raising Kids Who Read: What Parents and Teachers Can Do*. San Francisco,
CA: Jossey-Bass, 2015.

Wink, Joan. *The Power of Story*. Santa Barbara, CA: Libraries Unlimited, 2017.

Zooniverse. Zooniverse.org.